REFERENCE

RELATIONSHIPS BETWEEN SCORE
AND CHOREOGRAPHY
IN TWENTIETH-CENTURY DANCE

Music, Movement and Metaphor

Paul Hodgins

The Edwin Mellen Press
Lewiston/Queenston/Lampeter

Library of Congress Cataloging-in-Publication Data

Hodgins, Paul.
    Relationships between score and choreography in twentieth-century
dance : music, movement, and metaphor / Paul Hodgins.
        p.   cm.
    Includes bibliographical references and index.
    ISBN 0-7734-9552-5
    1. Music and dance. 2. Music--20th century--Philosophy and
aesthetics. 3. Dancing--Philosophy. 4. Ballets--20th century-
-Analysis, appreciation.   I. Title.
ML3858.H6 1992
792.8'2--dc20   92-10794
                                                            CIP
                                                            MN

A CIP catalog record for this book
is available from the British Library.

The Edwin Mellen Press   The Edwin Mellen Press
        Box 450   Box 67
    Lewiston, New York   Queenston, Ontario
        USA 14092   CANADA L0S 1L0

                The Edwin Mellen Press, Ltd.
                  Lampeter, Dyfed, Wales
                UNITED KINGDOM SA48 7DY

            Printed in the United States of America

RELATIONSHIPS BETWEEN SCORE AND CHOREOGRAPHY IN TWENTIETH-CENTURY DANCE

Music, Movement and Metaphor

Table of Contents

ACKNOWLEDGEMENTS

Dance scholarship is a mysterious and sometimes confusing realm for a musician. Fortunately, I was able to rely upon the kindness of many colleagues and friends who are much more knowledgeable than I am in their respective specialties.

At the University of California, Irvine, dance department colleagues Mary Corey and Dianne Howe provided me with invaluable advice and encouragement, and librarian Lorelei Tangei gave generously of her time. Grants from the University of California and the U. C. Irvine School of Fine Arts were crucial to the book's completion. At the University of Southern California, professor Bruce Brown must be singled out for special praise. He patiently read and advised from the very beginning, when chapters were mere outlines. At The Edwin Mellen Press, Barbara Jones was instrumental in convincing me to finish and submit the manuscript. At the Performing Arts Research Center of the New York Public Library, Madeleine M. Nichols provided dogged detective work. Lisa Macklin at the Dance Notation Bureau in New York helped locate valuable annotated manuscripts. Barbara Horgan of the Balanchine Trust, Alan Boehmer, and Patrice Whiteside were also extremely helpful.

Acknowledgement must be made to Boosey & Hawkes, Inc., and to the Dance Notation Bureau for the use of published scores and manuscripts as source material (although it should be noted that no score or manuscript excerpts were reproduced in any way; all musical examples have been retypeset, and include only those instrumental parts pertinent to the analysis at hand).

Highest praise is bestowed upon my wife, Anne, for her patience, her unwavering confidence in my sometimes wavering abilities, and above all her love.

INTRODUCTION

It is difficult to analyze a relationship that, to many, appears both as natural and as ineffable as the wind in the trees. Music and dance share certain fundamental characteristics of rhythm, structure and function so innately that it is difficult even to differentiate each discipline's method of realizing such elements. In most cultures dance is seldom performed without music.

Of course, a dance can exist without a score or other external aural signposts; but even then it often marks time to its own intrinsic drummer, the ghost of music, whether or not that music is apparent to an audience. Like music, dance exists in time, and movement events are ordered along that temporal axis in some manner of periodic recurrence, be it regular or irregular, fast or slow, obvious or invisible. Time is the unavoidable x-axis, the structural spine upon which all musical and choreographic events are ordered. The spiritual alliance of dance and music is apparent even in certain aspects of their respective vocabularies – phrase, breath, pause, tempo, pulse – not surprisingly, since both deal with movements of the body measured in time.

One could argue that many of these concepts are also found in drama: pulse, tempo and other time-related elements are an inextricable component of dramatic presentation. But drama deals primarily with components of tempo, whereas dance is also involved, just as inextricably, with musical meter, accent, and many other musical elements, some of them extremely subtle, all of them occurring interdependently and often simultaneously.

Many characteristics of one discipline can be reflected and amplified in the other. Direct and recurring relationships may be discovered in elements such as dynamics, texture, counterpoint, accent, theme, and melody. In fact, even concerning the constituents of larger formal structure – period, large-scale repetition, the architecture of entire movements – music and dance can also be closely allied.

Music has the ability to evoke complex emotions, associations, and metaphorical allusions which, when coupled with and augmented by movement, can convey wordless messages of great power and import. The death of the protagonist in *Orpheus*, the death of the antagonist in *Errand Into the Maze*, the evil entrances of the profiteer in *The Green Table* are all powerful and evocative narrative events, their effectiveness heightened through the use of carefully constructed music-movement relationships: repetition, thematic association, and the choreographer's and composer's ability to play on the viewer's pre-existing knowledge of archetypal characters, musical and choreographic conceits, and other elements. Likewise, abstract choreographic constructs – the acerbic, understated vocabulary of *Agon*, the strongly psychological characterizations of *Billy the Kid* – are firmly united, in matters of aesthetics, philosophy and execution, to their musical counterparts. Watching any of these works in silence would result in a profoundly different experience for the viewer.

This most sophisticated level of relationship recognition depends to a large extent on the viewer's degree of cultural associativeness. For example, a thorough knowledge of Orphic mythology is vital to appreciating the underlying subtleties of the relationships between music and movement in Stravinsky/Balanchine's *Orpheus*. Martha Graham's and Gian Carlo Menotti's *Errand Into the Maze* is difficult to interpret satisfactorily, taking both music and choreography into account, without an awareness of both the Minotaur myth and psychosexual symbolism. And the stridently pacifist message of *The Green Table* becomes poignant and prescient only when considered in its historical and cultural context. (The music-movement relationships in all of these works will be analyzed in later chapters.) Even the works of iconoclasts such as Merce Cunningham and John Cage require a comprehensive knowledge of the Western performing art aesthetic in order for the viewer to fully appreciate their rejection or reassessment of many of its elements.

On a deeper level, though, a powerful and universally recognizable symbiosis resonates through the music-movement relationship. As we shall see in the next chapter, unavoidable expectations regarding movement are subconsciously aroused in us by various types of musical information, often even controlling our perception of movement events as we watch a dance. This "first level" of music-movement relationships is much more pervasive, coloring the entire network of our perceptions regarding a dance, helping to form an impression of what we have seen, what we are seeing, even what has yet to be seen.

In the following chapters I have set myself a daunting and complex task: to expose, explore and define the many avenues of theory, philosophy and performance which dance and music share – their common bonds. I believe that choreographers and composers, while more than willing to acknowledge that such relationships exist, are guilty of neglect, leaving these vitally important affinities to form at an instinctive level, their potential completely unexplored; and that conscious and intelligent exploration, besides making their works more resonant and satisfying to the viewer, is crucial to our understanding of how dance as an art form affects us.

We will begin by investigating the "first level" of music-movement relationships, observing the effects on viewers of different kinds of music during a dance performance. Based on the supposition that music must have some subliminal effects on a viewer's perception of tempo, duration, movement quality, accent and other kinesthetic elements, we will examine the results of a survey which examines such relationships. Next we will embark on a short review of critical, aesthetic and theoretical writings concerning the dance-music relationship, examining points of contention, problems of cross-disciplinary communication, and previous attempts to define music-movement affinities. The tendencies thus observed will lead to the creation of a paradigm outlining various categories of affinity between music and choreography, or *choreomusical* relationships. This paradigm will then be applied in a series of analyses, concentrating on acknowledged masterworks created in the last sixty years. This analytical process will help to fine-tune the paradigm, defining its uses and limitations.

Of course, each observer and creator of dance follows his or her own long-formed instincts and prejudices, and we have all developed, for the most part quite unconsciously, our own methods of perceiving and ordering information about choreomusical relationships. Hopefully this study will prompt us to make a more careful appraisal of this fascinating and long-neglected element of dance, and will show us that there is much more to the marriage of dance and music than meets the eye and ear.

CHAPTER I

Isolating and Defining

Intrinsic Perceptual Relationships

Between Music and Movement

Before we can begin to examine the "second level" of consciously utilized affinities between music and dance, those which require a sophisticated and shared cultural literacy between creator and viewer, we must start at the bottom and define the "first level": when we watch a dance, what are our preconceptions regarding the relationships between what we see and what we hear?

As we shall see in the following chapter, there are longstanding aesthetic arguments concerning the ability of music to express extrinsic characteristics, such as motion, suspension and weight, which are crucial elements of movement. Many take the position that music possesses no inherent expressibility, and any referential characteristics it is claimed to exhibit are simply the result of culturally imposed prejudices. Others claim that music is, in fact, extragenerically referential by its very nature, and that this characteristic is not only a crucial component of our music-listening ethos, but a universal trait.

Putting aside this argument for the moment, let us try instead to identify the kinds of perceptual preconceptions we maintain – be they learned or innate – about movement as it relates to music.

To study this aspect of the music-movement relationship more closely, a simple experiment was devised and implemented at the University of California, Irvine in 1986. Four groups of people were asked to watch the same videotaped dance and then answer a brief questionnaire about the performance. The dance, a duet of about six minutes' duration, was carefully choreographed to be as featureless as possible in its most important characteristics. It was deliberately made amorphous, without strong indications of structure, motive, rhythm or prevailing speed (the tempo, in fact, varied). The choreography included little unison, though the counterpoint was almost never strictly canonic or even highly imitative in nature. Every attempt was made to keep the dance's movement landscape completely smooth – i. e., non-narrative, non-motivic and non-developmental. Though the duet consisted of a male and female dancer, the two figures were identically dressed in blue unitards against a stark white cyclorama and black marley floor, with bright neutral front, top and side lighting. The dancers seldom touched each other and made eye contact only infrequently; they performed simple walking, jumping and swinging motions in a calculatedly pedestrian, Cunninghamesque manner, neither hurried nor sluggish, but never at a single tempo.

The four groups of viewers consisted wholly of undergraduate university students, divided fairly evenly between dance majors and non-majors, all of them with varying degrees of dance experience. In all about 200 viewers were solicited, or approximately 50 in each group. Each person was questioned as to his or her dance background – type of training and number of years of experience as a dancer. Based on calculated averages, differences between groups were quite small: each group had an average of about 4.5 years of training (with a deviation of no more than 0.3 years in any one group). Disciplinary backgrounds in each group broke down as follows:

ballet:	58% (+ or - 5%)
jazz:	24% (+ or - 6%)
modern:	08% (+ or - 5%)
other:	10% (+ or - 4%)

Group one was, in effect, a control group: they viewed the videotape in silence, without any accompaniment whatsoever, in a quiet classroom. The other groups viewed the videotape with three sharply contrasting taped musical accompaniments, all of which matched or were tailored to the length of the videotaped performance. Group two listened to the final movement of Bach's Brandenburg Concerto No. 4, a highly contrapuntal, tightly and clearly structured vivace filled with many instances of melodic restatement and concertino/ripieno dialogue. Group three was given an adagio movement from a middle period Beethoven piano sonata, its structure and meter obfuscated by the extremely slow tempo, long phrases, and frequent complex suspensions. It is predominantly melodic and highly chordal in texture, with few points of clear imitation. Group four was exposed to a soundscape of my own design, highly dissonant, eventful, harsh, unstructured but somewhat contrapuntal, utilizing elements of *musique concrète* together with synthesized sounds. Its effect was calculated to be deliberately unsettling and disorienting. With each of the three accompaniments, any correspondences between musical and choreographic events were completely coincidental.

Each of these four viewing groups was given identical questionnaires. They were not, of course, informed of the real purpose of the questionnaire, and questions about the music were strictly avoided.

Question 1 ("How long was the dance?") concerned one of the most obvious assumptions about the effect of music on dance: that some quality of the music, possibly its prevailing tempo, would affect the viewer's perception about the length of the choreography.

The control group, which viewed the videotape in silence, showed a considerable degree of accuracy in its estimates. 35% of respondents in this group picked (c) (4 to 5 minutes); 30% correctly guessed (d) (5 to 6 minutes). There was a marked drop-off at each extreme – no one in group one thought the work was shorter than three minutes or longer than eight. Still, as a group they came up somewhat short of the mark.

Group two (the Bach group) showed the highest degree of accuracy: almost half the viewers in this group correctly identified (d), and another one-third selected (c) – a significantly more accurate result than any other group. There was a much sharper drop-off as well – only one-quarter of the group selected any answer other than (c) or (d).

Group three (the Beethoven group) seriously misjudged the length of the choreography, tending toward underestimation. Fully 15% thought the dance was only three to four minutes long – about half of its actual length. The largest portion – about one-third – picked (c). Only 29% correctly chose (d). About 12% were evenly divided between (f) or (g) – the only group of the four to go to this extreme as well.

Group four (the "dissonance" group) also erred considerably, but in the opposite direction. A surprising 41% chose (e) – longer than the actual dance. Almost 15% picked (f). This was the only group which significantly overestimated the length of the work.

Several plausible conclusions may be inferred from this information. It would seem that music of precise, metronomic regularity, such as the Bach, possibly results in a more time-attuned dance viewer. Music which by the irregularity of its pulse and rhythmic character distorts the passing of time, such as the accompaniment for groups three and four, results in less temporal certainty in the viewer. The languid, relatively eventless Beethoven caused a diminishment of perceived duration; the busy, event-filled synthetic score caused just the opposite effect: an augmentation of perceived duration.

Another area of obvious potential relationship is perceived tempo. Can the tempo of the music influence the viewer's perception of the tempo of the dance?

In response to question 2 ("What tempo was the dance?"), none of the groups perceived the dance as possessing a quick tempo; group one chose a medium tempo (c) by a huge margin of over 80%. However, there is an interesting drift away from such certainty with each of the other groups. 25% of group two opted for (d) (slow); this number rose to 35% in group three. In group four, a surprising 41% chose either (d) or (e) (very slow). Obviously, the tempo of the music and the complexity of musical events have some bearing on perceived movement tempo. Musical events are generally more temporally compressed than dance events, the former in effect stretching the perceived length of the latter by their relative density. Not surprisingly, silence would seem to allow for the truest measure of movement tempo, since dance events are not then subjected to subliminal comparison with music events.

Question 3 ("Was the tempo constant or varied?") produced some surprisingly disparate results. Group one, attuned completely to every nuance of the choreography's intrinsic rhythm and tempo, voted overwhelmingly in favor of (b) (varied). Group two succumbed to the relentlessly regular rhythm of the Bach accompaniment, choosing (a) (the same) by a 3 to 1 margin. Groups three and four were less certain: group three favored (b) in a 60/40 split and group four (faced with the meterless, confusing synthesized score) was evenly divided.

Clearly, music without a strongly emphasized and consistent tempo confuses the viewer's perception of the prevailing dance tempo, whereas silence creates a much more tempo-sensitive dance viewer. Music with a clear and regular tempo, however, such as the Bach, seems to manipulate the viewer's movement tempo perceptions to some degree.

Questions 4 and 5 concerned structure ("Could the dance be divided into sections? If so, how many?") The choreography, as mentioned, was carefully designed to appear seamless and unified. Interestingly, a large majority in each of the three music-accompanied groups saw the work as sectionalized – group two overwhelmingly so (92%), the other two groups less so (over one-third said "no" in group three, about one-quarter in group four). Again, a clear correspondence can be seen between musical and choreographic perceptions: the regularly phrased, multi-sectional Bach manipulated the viewers in group two into seeing more choreographic sections than did the less sectionalized music in groups three and four. In the control group, a majority of the respondents – 71% – saw the choreography as being seamless and non-divisible.

Question 6 concerned movement quality, with choices varying from "smooth and supple" (a) to "very sharp and angular" (e). Although musical influences are not as dramatic in this particular question, a significant minority in both groups two and four (18% and 14% respectively) chose "somewhat sharp and angular" (d), while no one in group one chose that response. In addition, respondents in group one favored the smooth end of the response spectrum slightly more. The formlessness, sudden fortissimos, and lack of clear pulse in the musical accompaniment to group three seem to have confused viewer perceptions concerning movement quality: this group showed the most polarization on this question (58% chose (d), 42% (b), with no responses for (c)).

Question 7 involved frequency of counterpoint, and the responses show a striking result: group two, given the most clearly contrapuntal music, saw the most incidences of counterpoint in the choreography (58% chose (d), "5 or more examples"). Next came group four (91% chose (c) or (d)); the counterpoint in the synthesized score is not as clearly imitative nor as frequent as in the Bach, but many sections of counterpoint do appear. In the control group, almost 28% chose either (a) (none) or (b) (one or two). In group three, the largely homophonic Beethoven resulted in similar observations: one-third of the viewers chose either (a) or (b). In all of groups two and four, only four people chose (a) or (b) – a very small minority. There is a directly proportional relationship between real musical counterpoint and perceived choreographic counterpoint, with clearly delineated Baroque imitative counterpoint achieving the most direct influence.

This small-scale and imperfect survey makes no attempt to be comprehensive. Obviously, more accurate and interesting information could be derived from a larger and more diversified group of respondents. Variations among viewers with varying degrees of dance experience and between groups from different cultural milieux would also add a vital perspective to the variety of responses. And the insurmountable problem of semantic barriers – the non-translatability of descriptive terms idiomatic to one discipline into another discipline – must be acknowledged and somehow weighed in the balance. Words such as "fast," "counterpoint" and "smooth" are inherently imprecise and highly subjective. All of these limitations make accurate categorization impossible. Nevertheless, certain observable tendencies do become apparent, and these would probably remain fairly consistent in a larger survey.

Perhaps some of these results may seem self-evident. Choreographers, after all, have always incorporated obvious textural and structural musical elements into their works – sometimes slavishly so – and such relationships have created certain expectations in us. And it is certainly plausible to assume that the viewer's general cultural indoctrination, together with his/her ingrained and subliminal tendencies toward sound-music associativeness, permits him/her to see even music-movement relationships which don't really exist – akin, perhaps, to an optical illusion or a card trick. We see what we want to see, what we expect to see, based in part on given aural stimuli.

What is most surprising is the degree to which these subliminal expectations permeate the entire spectrum of the dance viewer's observational aesthetic. Elements of length, tempo, structure, texture, even movement quality are all dictated to some degree by the music, even before a single movement has been choreographed. Choreographers may choose to work with or against these strong subliminal influences, but one thing is certain: in many different ways (only a few of which have been discovered in this brief survey), what we hear exerts a profound and inescapable influence over what we see.

CHAPTER II

Critical, Aesthetic and Theoretical Writings:

Contradictions, Controversies,

And The Beginnings of A Solution

Since the proliferation of aesthetic and critical writing about dance began in the nineteenth century, the small body of writing devoted to the relationships between dance and music has been riddled with opposing aesthetic philosophies and glaring contradictions. The only point upon which almost all writers agree is that relationships between the two disciplines do indeed exist. As for the exact nature of these relationships, their relative importance, or indeed their very desirability, there are wildly differing viewpoints.

The opinions of dancers, musicians and dance critics offer the most fascinating and consistently contradictory body of writing. Relying for the most part on personal creative, performance and observational experience, these writings reveal more than anything else the highly personal, individualized, and essentially ineffable nature of collaboration between dancers and musicians. Considered in this context, contradictions between artists are quite understandable.

Of more direct interest, perhaps, are comments by respected observers of the dance such as John Martin, Edwin Denby and others which attempt to establish from an observer's standpoint some general aesthetic principals which apply to dance and its relationship to music. Usually, though, these remarks are quite brief, lack comprehensiveness, eschew musical description or represent a comparatively minor component of a larger aesthetic statement.

Serious and scholarly aesthetic inquiries into the music-movement relationship have yielded some fruitful theories concerning its essentially metaphorical nature, in the sense that "metaphor" refers to an iconic connection between two entities which establishes an analogy between their structural and qualitative properties. Although these theories naturally differ, a pattern which tends toward explicative theorizing can be seen, particularly in aesthetic writings of the last twenty years.

The following survey has several intentions:

- to lay bare some of the most troubling points of controversy in the writings of dancers, musicians, and observers of the dance;

- to examine a few of the most germane serious inquiries by music philosophers and aestheticians into the metaphysical foundations governing dance-movement affinities;

- to discuss writings in closely related fields which may bring some additional light to the subject.

Hopefully such an examination should suggest a logical framework for a systematic, analytical approach to choreomusical analysis.

* * * * *

In 1849, fairly early in his career, Richard Wagner (in *The Art-Work of the Future*) identified dance, music and poetry as "three primeval sisters whom we see at once entwine their measures wherever the conditions necessary for art manifest themselves...each of the three partners, unlinked from the united chain and bereft thus of her own life and motion, can only carry on an artificially inbreathed and borrowed life.[1]" Yet Wagner offers no concrete suggestions concerning the successful integration of the various disciplines – it is left to the artists themselves, presumably, to work out the fine points of this magical, synergistic interdisciplinary fusion described

---

[1]Richard Wagner, "The Art-Work of the Future" (1849), *What Is Dance?*, ed. Roger Copeland and Marshal Cohen (Oxford: Oxford University Press, 1983) 191, 192.

(rather floridly) by the composer. Others have grumbled that Wagner himself gave frustratingly short shrift to both dance and poetry in his own grandiose attempts at *Gesamtkunstwerk.* Eduard Hanslick, the nineteenth-century Viennese music critic perhaps best known for his determinedly anti-Wagnerian views, argued that grandiose attempts at synthesis between the performing arts only weakened music's inherent expressive powers.[2]

Among twentieth-century choreographers, composers, dance writers and critics, discussions concerning the nature of dance-music relationships resolve few differences of opinion; as might be expected, there is strong disagreement about the degree and types of interdependence music and choreography should have. Nowhere is the conflict more noticeable than in discussions pertaining to elements of gesture and texture. In his essay "Music and Action," composer Constant Lambert complains:

> There seems to be a growing theory that dancing which represents visually the formal devices and texture of the music must of necessity be pleasing to the musical mind. Nothing could be further from the truth. I am sure there must be innumerable musicians beside myself who experience the same feeling of exasperation when the choreographer turns the stage into a vast lecturer's blackboard and, by associating certain dancers with certain themes, proceeds to underline obvious formal devices in the music which any one of average intelligence can appreciate with half an ear. Literal translations from one language into another are always unsatisfactory and usually ridiculous...the choreographer is debasing his art if he thus makes dancing a mere visual expose of the music. The dance should not be a translation of the music but an interpretation of it. It should not slavishly imitate the musical texture but should add a counter-subject of its own.[3]

Lambert goes on to praise George Balanchine as "one of the few choreographers with the intelligence to realize that visual complexity is not

---

[2]Eduard Hanslick, *The Beautiful in Music,* trans. Gustav Cohen, 7th ed. (New York: Liberal Arts Press, 1957) viii.

[3]Constant Lambert, "Music and Action," Copeland and Cohen 208-09.

the most suitable accompaniment to aural complexity."[4] One wonders how Mr. Lambert would justify Balanchine's musically attentive approach to the score of Bach's *Concerto for Two Violins* in *Concerto Barocco*, for example, or how he would have responded to respected dance critic Edwin Denby's own reaction to the work:

> Balanchine has set his ballet so happily to Bach's *Concerto for Two Violins* that the score may be called his subject matter...in its vigorous dance rhythm, its long-linked phrases, its consistent drive and sovereign articulation, *Concerto Barocco* corresponds brilliantly to this masterpiece of Baroque music.[5]

This brings us to our first important controversy: the debate concerning music visualization, or the degree to which choreography and score reflect each other on a literal, ostensible level, in matters of gesture, rhythm, dynamic and texture.

Composer Louis Horst, Martha Graham's longtime collaborator, warns against overly literal correspondences:

> It is not necessary for the music to fit the dance like a glove; in fact, it should not fit too tightly...while the choreographer should not follow the music slavishly, there must be synthesis between dance and accompaniment.[6]

Doris Humphrey makes a similar statement in *The Art of Making Dances* :

> ...the dance is an independent art, subject to laws of its own which can lead the choreographer to movements not readily indicated in the score at all....The dance must have something to say of its own, and a mere visualization of the music is not sufficient justification for bringing it to birth.[7]

Yet Humphrey offers no alternative to "mere visualization"; nor does Horst explain what this "synthesis between dance and accompaniment" might entail

---

[4]Lambert 209.

[5]Edwin Denby, "A Balanchine Masterpiece, "*Looking at the Dance* (New York: Pellegrini & Cudahy, 1949) 125. Unfortunately, Denby describes music-movement correspondences in purely kinesthetic fashion, without reference to the score, and he avoids musical terminology entirely: he writes only of the "weight" and "stress" of the music (125, 126).

[6]*Dance Perspectives* 16 (1963): 10.

[7]Doris Humphrey, *The Art of Making Dances* (New York: Rinehart & Co., 1959) 135, 137.

(his advice also hints of musical subservience). It is difficult to reconcile such remarks with Denby's, or with Stravinsky's observation that "[t]here should be no discordance between the movements of the dance and the imperative demands that the measure of the music imposes."[8] Suffice to say that the degree of music visualization in dance depends to a large extent upon both the choreographer's own predilections and the translatability into movement gestures of the musical topography involved.

Problems concerning the relative duration of kinesthetic and musical gestures have created intractable philosophical disagreements. When asked his opinion of Balanchine's and Stravinsky's collaborative aesthetic, John Cage replied:

> I have never been satisfied with the Balanchine-Stravinsky collaborations which have been dependent on making ten fingers seem to be like two feet, which is impossible.[9]

This observation, so pithy, astute and typically Cageian, forces us to consider a truism overlooked, or at least unacknowledged, by countless choreographers and composers: the fundamental incompatibility of music's and dance's gestural tempi. String tremolos, woodwind arpeggios, and piano trills are all highly idiomatic and widely used musical devices, the quintessential ingredients of musical gesture. They are, of course, executed primarily by actions of the fingers, wrists and forearms. Yet even relatively small gestures in dance involve feet, arms, lower legs, and the head – larger body parts, hence larger and more time-consuming gestures. Or as Cage put it: "Fingers don't use the same time-lengths legs do. It's the difference between two and ten."[10]

This small-scale durational disparity creates pervasive temporal consequences all the way up the structural hierarchy. In music, the length and shape of the phrase is dependent on instrumentally idiomatic elements, such as the length and speed of the string player's bow or the force and

---

[8]*Dance Perspectives* 16: 9.

[9]Richard Kostelanetz, *Conversing with Cage* (New York: Limelight Editions, 1988) 192.

[10]*Dance Perspectives* 16: 40.

duration of the wind player's breath. To the dancer these units of musical measurement may seem arbitrary or irrelevant, but to the composer and instrumentalist they are immutable musical standards, age-old and completely intrinsic to the discipline. In dance, the phrase's shape and length is determined by a much larger and less temporally precise instrument – the body in motion, within the confines of the stage or studio. An *enchaînement* combination moving across the floor or a series of slow *pas de bourées* are often referred to as a single dance phrase. Any dance accompanist knows that such "phrases" have little to do with phrases of music. The movement phrase frequently translates into a larger musical structure: the duration of a period, say, or even an entire section in simple binary form.

John Martin represents one side of another aesthetic argument in his discussion of the choreographic use of fugal techniques:

> "...in dances designed to be seen by spectators, [the fugue] is a device that can be used only incidentally and at some risk. Highly contrapuntal arrangements in any medium demand great mental concentration from an audience, and so much so in the dance that they are generally conducive of little besides visual confusion."[11]

Yet, as we shall see in the following analyses, the works of Balanchine, Loring and others are filled with examples of closely corresponding musical and choreographic fugue and other overt textural parallels.[12] There must be some aspect of their choreographic craft, therefore, which renders their use of these devices acceptable (or so well-integrated to the musical architecture as to be unnoticeable) to the ever-observant Mr. Martin.

Concerning perhaps the most basic music-movement correspondence, that of rhythm, we find similar disagreements. In his essay "Notes on Music and Dance," composer Steve Reich states that "...the basic impulse at the foundation of all dance [is] the human desire for regular rhythmic movement,

---

[11]John Martin, "Form and Composition," *Introduction to the Dance* (1939; New York: Dance Horizons, 1968) 82.

[12]Balanchine describes his literal choreographic use of a two-voice fugue from the score of *Elegie* in "The Dance Element in Stravinsky's Music," *Stravinsky in the Theatre*, ed. Minna Lederman (1949; New York: Da Capo, 1975) 77.

usually done to music."[13] He then makes an impassioned plea for the return of rhythm as an integral choreomusical relationship. His stand can be better appreciated, perhaps, when considered in its historical context: immediately after the culmination of the era of Cunningham-Cage experimentalism (the early 1970's), he undoubtedly felt that modern dance had lost touch with the rhythmic origins of the discipline. His own then-recent studies of West African folk music, so highly rhythmic and inextricably bound to ancient dance traditions, would undoubtedly have contributed to this belief.

George Balanchine, writing a generation earlier, voiced a similar opinion regarding the choreographic importance of rhythm when discussing the music of Stravinsky:

> Stravinsky's strict beat is his sign of authority over time; over his interpreters too. A choreographer should, first of all, place confidence without limit in this control...A choreographer can't invent rhythms, he only reflects them in movement. The body is his medium and, unaided, the body will improvise for a short breath. But the organizing of rhythm on a grand scale is a sustained process. It is a function of the musical mind.[14]

Composer Gunther Schuller remarked that watching "a choreography which consistently ignores the metric...shapes of the music...is like reading a book in which the printer has put all the commas and periods in the middle of sentences and clauses."[15]

It is difficult to reconcile the opinions of Reich, Balanchine and Schuller with the advice of John Martin:

> It is wise when considering rhythm in the dance to put aside all preconceptions deriving from musical rhythm. The latter, it is true, originates at the same source, namely, the natural movement of the body, but as music has been developed as an absolute art, its relation to bodily experience has become increasingly attenuated until in many instances it approaches the point of disappearance.[16]

---

[13]Steve Reich, "Notes on Music and Dance," *Ballet Review* 4.5 (1973): 68.

[14]Balanchine 75.

[15]*Dance Perspectives* 16: 37.

[16]Martin 67-8. Mr. Martin seems to be confusing the concepts of *rhythm* and *gesture*.

Adds composer Vivian Fine:

> In modern dance it is not the metrical aspects of rhythm that
> unite dance and music. In the free interweaving of movement
> and sound there is a link to deeper rhythm. Free of superficial
> points of rhythmic contact, music and dance create patterns of
> inter-relatedness that enhance the total work.[17]

Martin and Fine both imply an excellent point, and one overlooked by
Reich in his somewhat oversimplistic polemic: like musical gestures, the
rhythms of much contemporary Western art music often have very little to do
with the gross body rhythms associated with dance movement. Particularly
since the advent of instrumental virtuosity in the last two centuries, elements
of musical phrasing, gesture, rhythm and cadence have all accelerated to the
point where they frequently bear no semantic correspondence to their
choreographic counterparts, further exacerbating the fundamental temporal
disparity between music and dance, pushing their time-based parameters
even further apart. Add to that the increasingly complex and free use of
mixed meters in much Western art music of the last ninety years, and the
dissolution of meter in much mid-twentieth-century music, and the successful
applicability of Reich's rhythmic aesthetic to contemporary music and dance
seems remote.

Another fundamental element of both music and dance, namely
structure, has been the subject of wildly differing opinions when its cross-
disciplinary applicability is discussed. Louis Horst and his followers
considered his lectures on the pre-Classic dance forms to be elementary
courses in formal dance composition.[18] He believed that musical structure
"helps the dance by confining it, as a frame confines a painting. It provides a
disciplinary measure for the choreographer, and it deepens the meaning of
the dance for the spectator."[19] John Martin, on the other hand, viewed
traditional musical structures as anathema to choreographers:

---

[17]*Dance Perspectives* 16: 9.

[18]See Henry Gilfond, foreword, *Pre-Classic Dance Forms,* by Louis Horst (1937; New York:
Dance Horizons, 1972) viii-ix.

[19]*Dance Perspectives* 16: 8.

Logically enough, when the more progressive choreographer first sees the need for breaking away from this hampering dependence upon music, he is more than likely to take with him as his basis for independent composition those practices which he automatically acquired from the musician. By reason of this inertia, it is the frequent procedure of dancers, even when composing entirely without the aid of music, to follow musical formulas, in spite of the fact that the forms devised specifically to solve musical problems are generally unsuitable to dance....Materials play so vital a part in the shaping of form that the application of any of these common principals to music and to dance produces quite different results, and there is actually no formal unity between them.[20]

On this point Stravinsky and Martin are in agreement. Said Stravinsky, "Choreography, as I conceive it, must realize its own form, independent of the musical form though measured to the musical unit."[21] (Notice, though, that Stravinsky maintains a firm conviction regarding the necessity of close rhythmic correspondences.)

To Cage and Cunningham, traditional music-movement structural correspondences were an aesthetic dead-end to be avoided. Said Cage:

...in working with Merce, the first thing we did was to liberate the music from the necessity to go with the dance, and to free the dance from having to interpret the music...I...established a rhythmic structure for the music...based on the square root [thus enabling Cage to connect large-scale and small-scale structural events with proportional number series]...and then Merce would make a dance within that structure. I would make music within the same structure, and then the two would come together without in any way having forced each other in terms of details....Then as my work continued, I gave up the need for structure by getting involved in process, and the dance was free to be in that process. The result is now two things that are not at all even structured the same way can go together.[22]

Cage's approach represents the logical conclusion of the increasing abstraction to which the dance-music relationship was subjected in the first three postwar decades. The correspondence has been distilled to its

---

[20]Martin 78.

[21]*Dance Perspectives* 16: 35.

[22]Kostelanetz 192.

metaphysical baseline, the often indiscernible relationship of process, and little concern is shown for the visibility of the result.

As the preceding chapter made clear, though, we *tend* to see correspondences between music and dance; and these relationships, whether intentionally conceived or not, are both consciously and unconsciously perceived by the viewer. Composer Gunther Schuller makes this point in his refutation of the Cage-Cunningham aesthetic of disciplinary autonomy:

> Some claim that the dance must be "autonomous." Quite apart from the semantic ambiguity of such a term, is it really possible for a dance movement to be autonomous of the music to which it is set? Somehow at the most fundamental level – and therefore precisely the most important, internal level – the choreographer receives some degree of stimulus from the music, and no matter to what extent he wishes to disguise this relationship, it is an inextricable part of the whole. The only truly "autonomous" dance is one which is unaccompanied.[23]

Underlying and informing all of these arguments is a controversy of philosophical rather than practical importance, but one which nonetheless exerts a profound influence on each choreographer's or composer's own collaborative aesthetic: the relative importance of the two disciplines in the final *Gesamtkunstwerk,* and the question of disciplinary dominance. Which is the controlling art form, music or dance? Should the influence of each discipline even be considered separately? At what point and in what form must concessions be made? Louis Horst uses an interesting image in his description of the process of disciplinary balance:

> ...the dance should be the center of interest, the point of tension. The music should be transparent, open and spacious, so the audience can see through it. If the music is thick and overloaded, as it is apt to be if it was written to be heard alone, it obscures the dance.[24]

Horst's views exemplify the sentiments of a wide array of choreographers and composers, too disparate in their aesthetics to be termed a school, who could be termed literalists. Believing the dance-music relationship to be largely gestural in nature, they reason that an overabundance of musical events

---

[23]*Dance Perspectives* 16: 36-37.

[24]*Ibid.* 16: 6.

provides excessive gestural material for the choreographer. This aesthetic presupposes the overwhelming necessity for movement to reflect music in a literal, gestural fashion, and dismisses the interpretative possibilities of non-literal choreomusical relationships, deliberate contrasts between choreography and score, or even extrinsic references.

Concerning the predominance of either music or dance, opinions are split, not surprisingly, according to the discipline of the artist. Composer Norman Dello Joio doubts the inherent interpretive strength of dance alone:

> Dance may not be a lesser art, but it has no life of its own disassociated from music. It derives its stimulus from music. I am aware that some people hold the opposite view – that music should be inspired by the dance for which it is written. As a composer, I take serious exception to this. Though it is possible for a composer to write this way, I doubt that the resultant score can have much musical merit.[25]

But musical merit, argues Susanne Langer, is irrelevant when evaluating the effectiveness of music within the context of *Gesamtkunstwerk* :

> A dance is not necessarily the better for using very good music. Dance normally swallows music, as music normally swallows words. The music that, perhaps, first inspires a dance, is none the less cancelled out as art in its own right, and assimilated to the dance; and for this many a third-rate musical piece has served as well as a significant work.[26]

Those of us who have suffered through the scores of Minkus or Adam in concert can readily attest to the truthfulness of the last part of Langer's remarks, even if we disagree with the first part. Her belief in a disciplinary hierarchy, moreover, is supplemented by a theory of disciplinary dominance: "Every work has its primary apparition, to which all other virtual dimensions are secondary. There are no happy marriages in art – only successful rape."[27] According to Langer, egalitarian collaboration is an arbitrary and ultimately pointless process, and one discipline or the other will inevitably be relegated to the role of subservience.

---

[25]*Ibid.*, 16: 18.

[26]Susanne K. Langer, *Problems of Art* (New York: Charles Scribner's Sons, 1957) 84-5.

[27]Langer 86.

The most common issue in these writings concerns the problem of prolonged obviousness in the choreomusical partnership. There seems to be a definite consensus among many observers of the dance, regardless of their disciplinary affiliation, that meaningful long-term dance-music relationships cannot exist solely on the level of imitation, the overt and constant choreographic mirroring of meter, rhythm, dynamic, texture and other musical elements – even if they disagree on the importance of those elements in a more localized, moment-to-moment context. The genius of Balanchine's use of music, argues musician Kenneth LaFave, is his deliberate avoidance of sustained or overly obvious correspondences. They are saved by the choreographer for "epiphanic moments" only.[28] LaFave describes Balanchine's choreography as "the dancers in a dialogue with the score, rather than in imitation of it...it isn't a matter of a certain kind of sound translating into a certain kind of step, but of a composition's inner workings being grasped by the choreographer and infused into the dance."[29] But these observations naturally raise some difficult questions: What is the nature of this "dialogue"? How does it differ from mere imitation? What elements of a composition could be considered its "inner workings" as opposed to obvious (and thus less choreographically attractive) surface characteristics? Are all imitative relationships inherently bad? Does the deliberate avoidance of overt choreomusical imitation by itself impel us to see deeper relationships, even where they don't exist?

It would be monumentally difficult and ultimately pointless to extract some neat and tidy conclusions from this morass of conflicting observations and questions; one thing that may be stated unequivocally, however, is that many writers critically or creatively associated with dance talk freely and disagree fundamentally about dance-music affinities without ever precisely defining the nature or parameters of those affinities. Yet out of the ambiguities of imprecise terms and ill-defined concepts, one can begin to discern several types of choreomusical affinity emerging; and that dance-

---

[28]Kenneth LaFave, "Point Counterpoint," *Ballet News* (June 1983): 25.

[29]LaFave 25, 26.

music relationships must exist also on a more subliminal, less obviously imitative level. It would be useful, therefore, to identify and categorize these relationships more accurately from a viewer's perspective, then apply this method of categorization to comprehensive music-movement analyses to prove its efficacy. Only by establishing a common evaluative system will it be possible to argue intelligently about the many important issues surrounding the dance-music relationship. Perhaps the theories of scholars in the fields of musical aesthetics and philosophy will help bring us closer to that goal.

*   *   *   *   *

Eduard Hanslick identified the nature of the relationship between music and extramusical events as follows:

> A certain class of ideas...is quite susceptible of being adequately expressed by means which unquestionably belong to the sphere of music proper. This class comprises all ideas which...are associated with audible changes of strength, motion, and ratio: the ideas of intensity waxing and diminishing; of motion hastening and lingering...all these ideas being expressible by corresponding modifications of sound.[30]

This, of course, was not a radically new observation even then (it can be traced back at least to Aristotle's *Poetics*), and the controversy surrounding the very expressibility of music, its ability to signify any property or thing other than itself, rages on to this day.[31] I believe that the conclusions derived from the survey described in the last chapter, however, argue strongly in favor of Hanslick's theory. Unfortunately we must ignore this important controversy within the limited context of the present study, accepting the

---

[30]Hanslick 22-23

[31]The imitative qualities of music concerning motion are discussed by eighteenth-century British philosopher James Harris in *Three Treatises: the First Concerning Art; the Second Concerning Music, Painting and Poetry; the Third Concerning Happiness,* 3rd ed. (London, 1772) 65-67. Igor Stravinsky, however, argues that "music, by its very nature, is essentially powerless to *express* anything at all, whether a feeling, an attitude of mind, a psychological mood, a phenomenon of nature, etc....Expression has never been an inherent property to music." (Stravinsky, *Chronicle of My Life* [London: Victor Gollancz, 1936] 91.) See also Peter Kivy, "Music as Imitation," *Sound and Semblance* (Princeton University Press, 1984) 3-18.

reality that many choreographers claim to utilize music's expressive properties without first defining their exact nature, often making their interpretation of the music's emotional content clearer through the narrative and expressive elements of their own choreography.

The properties of musical expression which enable it to be perceived iconically on a metaphorical level are labelled extrageneric musical meanings by Wilson Coker, a contemporary aesthetic theorist. He defines extrageneric musical meanings as those resultants of a primarily iconic sign situation in which someone interprets a musical work or some portion of it as a sign of some apparently non-musical object.[32] Writers such as Coker and, even more recently, Peter Kivy, examine closely the various metaphorical qualities relating to motion which music has been frequently credited to possess. On the whole, Coker has developed a theory of music-movement isomorphism which accepts *a priori* the existence of extrageneric meanings. Insists Coker:

> ...an important purpose of musical gestures, though many aestheticians and musicians forget this simple fact, is to deal with matters other than musical gestures. [The] other aesthetic purpose of music is to deal with non-musical things.[33]

Coker goes on to list the many qualities of motion and emotion which music can easily signify – tempo, calmness, excitement, tenseness, agitation, violence, and so forth – pointing out that these are "characteristic qualities that all things in motion may have in various degrees....We may interpret music as the metaphor for...organic behavior especially."[34]

Coker actually presents a brief analysis of a scene from a ballet, the final "Pas D'Action" from Stravinsky/Balanchine's *Orpheus*, beginning his examination with a statement which by now his argument has made abundantly clear:

> The musical presentation of metaphors for bodily gestures is, we recognize, an essential function of music for the dance...in

---

[32]Wilson Coker, *Music and Meaning: A Theoretical Introduction* (New York: The Free Press, 1972) 61, 144.

[33]Coker, 151.

[34]Coker, 157.

> ballet music...musical gestures significantly refer to the
> character of...such organic sounds as running, lunging, striking
> out, and so forth.[35]

The analysis is rich with musical detail and excerpts from the score, but strangely lacking in detailed choreographic description. Nor does Coker attempt to differentiate clearly between different types of extrageneric signification, despite the fact that the categories of metaphorical relationship with which he concludes his analysis clearly include two distinctly different types of choreomusical metaphor:

    1) a prevailing emotional attitude of anger and violence;

    2) gestures of attack;

    3) an abrupt seizure;

    4) a tearing into pieces.[36]

The first category concerns emotional metaphor; the other three are primarily gestural. Clearly, any effective paradigm for the delineation of isomorphic choreomusical relationships must make distinctions between these two broad areas.

    Musician and music educator Emile Jaques-Dalcroze, who in the late nineteenth century developed a system of kinesthetic exercises for musicians which he called eurhythmics, recognized that choreomusical relationships can involve extrinsic elements. In his essay "Music and the Dancer" Jaques-Dalcroze noted that:

> There is an intimate connection between sound and gesture,
> and the dance that is based on music should draw its
> inspiration at least as much, and even more, from its subjective
> emotions as from its external rhythmic forms.[37]

Again, we are faced with the problem of elucidating the difference between gestural relationships and those based upon extrinsic elements (i.e. those which lie outside strictly literal choreomusical correspondence), such as "subjective emotions."

---

[35]Coker, 160.

[36]Coker, 164.

[37]Emile Jaques-Dalcroze, "Music and the Dancer," *Rhythm, Music and Education* (New York: The Knickerbocker Press, 1921) 296.

Jaques-Dalcroze recognizes additional categories of intrinsic choreomusical relationship which Coker fails to identify: the establishment of thematic relationships between movement and music through repetition and development, for example, or textural relationships involving the correspondence of instrumental and choreographic "thickness."[38] Yet nowhere are these relationships described in anything more than tangential fashion; and again the distinction between intrinsic and extrinsic choreomusical affinities remains blurred, their important differences unacknowledged.

Certainly none of these writers has presented a convincing and comprehensive theory explaining music-movement relationships. Yet aesthetic theorists such as Kivy and Coker and pedagogical theorists such as Jaques-Dalcroze are all making sincere attempts to address, in a rational way, the underlying aesthetic issues which govern our perception of these relationships – something that few dance writers have been able to do. Using their observations as a point of departure, we can now begin to fashion a set of criteria which circumscribe this confusing collection of music-movement affinities.

---

[38]See Jaques-Dalcroze 295, 303.

CHAPTER III

A Paradigm for Choreomusical Analysis

As the preceding survey makes clear, any successful system of choreomusical analysis must satisfy a number of different criteria. A distinction must be made between those relationships which exist intrinsically and those which involve an extrinsic referent; subcategories within each of these broad areas must be defined; internal correspondences must include rhythmic and textural parallels at the minimum; finally, parameters and limitations must be determined (this last element will undoubtedly be developed through application rather than initial prediction).

Let us begin the formation of a paradigm with a definition of these two broad categories:

Intrinsic relationships emanate from the realms of musical and kinesthetic gesture. They involve the iconic cross-disciplinary reflection of highly ostensible and idiomatic elements, their interpretation largely unprejudiced by context.

Extrinsic relationships admit the presence of an implied third partner to the choreomusical marriage – an external element such as a characterization or narrative event which is acknowledged in some way by both music and choreography.

Let us now examine these two broad categories and their various sub-categories in a greater magnitude of detail. I will refrain at this point from providing examples from the repertoire to illustrate each category of relationship, relying instead upon their effective application in the six choreomusical analyses.

Intrinsic relationships do not depend upon context – a foreknowledge of the narrative of the ballet, a shared cultural ethos between artists and audience, or other preconceptions. They are often quite easy to observe. These correspondences fall into five categories:

A. Rhythmic
   1. Accent and meter: accent patterns in the score, whether metrical or syncopated, are paralleled by a corresponding movement accent;
   2. Movement/score integration: sounds produced by the dancer or dancers (hand claps, foot stomps, etc.) are an integrated rhythmic element of the score.

B. Dynamic: The volume of the musical gesture is matched by the size of the choreographic gesture (usually occurring as part of another choreomusical correspondence).

C. Textural
   1. Instrumental vs. choreographic forces: the number of instruments and dancers are roughly equivalent: a solo instrument with a solo dancer, a duet with a *pas de deux*, a large ensemble for a *corp* section;
   2. Homophonic/polyphonic affinities: the choreography reflects the degree of homophony or polyphony in the score – unison group movement for homophony, variegated movement for polyphony;
   3. Counterpoint: the reflection of canonic or highly imitative music in the choreographic structure.

D. Structural: Correspondences of structure can be observed within the following units of musical syntax:

1. Motive/Figure;
2. Phrase/Period;
3. Larger structures.

E. Qualitative

1. Tessitura: the degree of perceived highness or lowness of a passage of music is reflected by an appropriate choreographic parallel, such as pointework or heavy, grounded movement;

2. Timbre: a parallel is established between a dancer or group of dancers and a specific instrument or family of instruments.

Often timbral relationships are sex-based: the use of brass choirs for male group sections, for example, or woodwind choirs for female group sections;

3. Degree of sharpness/smoothness: staccato or legato passages in the music are reflected by sharp or sustained movements;

4. Degree of dissonance/consonance: the level of dissonance or consonance in the music's harmonic language is choreographically acknowledged.

F. Mimetic

1. Instrumental imitation: a dancer mimes instrumental performance, the appropriate sound being provided by the score;

2. Non-instrumental imitation: a dancer mimes a sound-associated movement event, such as a shout or the loud report of a gun, and a corresponding mimetic instrumental effect is provided in the score.

Extrinsic relationships depend largely upon narrative and cultural context – the shared knowledge of the ballet's characters and plot (if any), as well as the audience's pre-knowledge of pertinent sociological, psychological and mythological information, are crucial to their recognition and appreciation. They often share the characteristics of some intrinsic relationships. These correspondences fall into three categories:

> *A. Archetypal*: a musical theme, texture or instrumentation and a corresponding prescribed movement phrase or vocabulary are associated with archetypal characters or themes;

> *B. Emotional/Psychological*: the score and choreography reflect the emotional and/or psychological state of an individual character or group; often used as a foreshadowing device;

> *C. Narrative*: the music and movement help to depict an important element or event of the plotline in a narrative choreography.

Any choreomusical relationship may be presented in one of three temporal alignments:

> 1) Direct: musical and choreographic elements are presented simultaneously;
> 2) Foreshadowing: either musical or choreographic element is introduced separately, followed by direct presentation;
> 3) Reminiscence: either musical or choreographic element is reiterated alone after direct presentation.

Obviously, this paradigm invites debate, particularly in issues such as the literalness of the extrinsic categories. A case could be made for labelling the first category of extrinsic relationship "imitative" and the last two "expressive." I have decided, however, to avoid the difficulty of defining those loaded, ambiguous terms, particularly considering the interpretive ballast associated with "expressive" dance and the age-old arguments surrounding music's "imitative" nature.

Several points need to be stressed at the outset:

– It is entirely possible, and indeed quite common, for a given passage of dance to contain several simultaneous categories of choreomusical relationship.

– Any choreomusical relationship can assume *thematic* significance only through repetition and development. It is not itself a separate category of relationship, but a natural result of sustained correspondences.

– We will see many instances when obvious intrinsic affinities are deliberately avoided, particularly at points when such a correspondence would seem predictable or overly labored, or, more rarely, when we have been led to expect the return of a pre-established relationship. Frequently, however, subtle extrinsic affinities can be found at points where no apparent intrinsic relation-ship exists.

– The paradigm allows small distinctions to be made. For example, the sixteenth note legato passages in the first movement of Mozart's *Sonata Facile*, K.545, for solo piano could yield quite different results when paired with two different types of balletic movement:

– with *petits battements frappés* performed by a *corp* we would see a rhythmic and dynamic parallel but a textural and qualitative contrast;

– with a large, sustained *arabesque* performed by a soloist we would see a rhythmic and dynamic contrast but a textural and qualitative parallel.

In applying this paradigm, my goals are modest. It is intended as an analytical tool only, and a narrowly focussed one at that. Any comprehensive examination of a dance masterwork must include many other realms of inquiry, involving the choreographer's intent, influences, choreographic vocabulary, and innumerable other factors.

Nevertheless, it is my belief that in the greatest masterworks, choreographies such as *Apollon Musagète, Orpheus, Agon, Billy the Kid, The Green Table*, and *Errand Into the Maze*, a complex and all-pervading network of choreomusical constructs can be uncovered through the careful application of this model, and that few, if any, moments of choreography are completely unconnected to the score. In such works, music and dance are united in a common and continuous expressive language, no one element of which would be complete when considered outside of its choreomusical context. True, in some of these works, obvious intrinsic relationships are used sparingly; but always, if the paradigm is rigorously applied, other choreomusical connections of wonderful subtlety and ingenuity may be found.

In choosing six masterworks for analysis, I decided first of all to examine only those works in which complete and thorough collaboration between choreographer and composer was achieved (the only exception, *Apollon Musagete*, merits inclusion partly because of the special and longstanding relationship between Balanchine and Stravinsky, and because of its profound influence on the former's subsequent relationship with the music of the latter). I chose only those works in which I felt music and dance seemed to play equal interpretive and expressive roles; I focussed on choreographies of the last seventy years, the era since the iconoclastic productions of the *Ballets Russes* in which the two disciplines have struggled toward a more or less equitable co-existence. This selection of analyses is regrettably small; more recent works are, unfortunately, omitted. Hopefully, others will find many more dance works worthy of some form of choreomusical analysis.

CHAPTER IV

The Balanchine-Stravinsky Partnership

Among the collaborative artistic partnerships of this century, that of Igor Stravinsky and George Balanchine occupies a special place. For its enduring popularity, its consistency of craftsmanship, the subtlety of its music-movement relationships, its style, craft, and vision, their output remains unequalled. Three principal masterworks stand alone, and will be subjected to choreomusical analysis here: *Apollon Musagète* (1928) (sometimes called *Apollo* in subsequent years, but here referred to by its original name), *Orpheus* (1948), and *Agon* (1957).

Several factors, coupled with fortunate circumstances, informed the Stravinsky-Balanchine partnership. Both men shared a vibrant and priviliged culture – pre-Soviet Russia; specifically, the world of the *fin de siècle* Imperial Russian cultural and intellectual elite. Though separated by a generation, they were nonetheless equally imbued with a single and singular cultural ethos, that of Imperial Russia. Both were raised and educated in St. Petersburg, the most European of Russian cities. Said Vera Stravinsky: "the life in St. Petersburg, the artistic life, was very special. Everybody knew each other. They met, they criticized....everybody want[ed] to be an artist in literature, or ballet, in the theatre, painting..."[1] Both men were itinerant for

---

[1]Genevieve Oswald, "Vera Stravinsky Interview," Transcript of Oral History Project, 14 June 1976, New York City Public Library, Dance Collection: 3.

long periods of time, becoming steeped in western European (particularly French) cultural influences. Both eventually became famous expatriates living in America, arriving within a few years of each other. Both enjoyed critical and popular acclaim from an early age. Both were quietly religious. And both adhered, through many years of professional and personal affiliation, to the Apollonian aesthetic ideal of restraint, objectivity, balance and well-crafted elegance in their work. Lincoln Kirstein defines their shared roots as:

> a common metaphysic. Icon and liturgy in Greek Orthodoxy inherited from Byzantium are their roots...[t]hey represent a non-romantic type of twentieth-century "maker" (rather than "creator").[2]

It could be argued, of course, that Balanchine's mature choreography exhibits these traits at least partly because of the influence of the forceful and inspiring guidance of Stravinsky, 22 years his senior. After all, Balanchine was only 24 and close to the beginning of his career when he was first thrust, quite unexpectedly, into a collaborative role with the composer, then already long-famous and enormously influential. And he was an acknowledged mentor. Balanchine had first been exposed to Stravinsky's music in 1915, as an eleven-year-old supernumerary in the opera *Le Rossignol*. Four years later, he set three excerpts from the *Pulcinella* suite. In 1921, he attempted (and failed) to mount a production of *Le Sacre du Printemps*; and in 1924 he was asked by Diaghilev to choreograph a ballet to the music of *Le Rossignol*.

Of Stravinsky's influence, Balanchine comments: "Stravinsky's effect on my own work has always been in the direction of control, of simplification and quietness."[3] Indeed, Balanchine's approach to the choreographic treatment of music owes an incalculable debt to the composer.[4] The

[2]Nancy Lassalle, ed., "Stravinsky and Balanchine: Fifty Years of Partnership: 1920-1971" (New York: New York City Ballet, 1971) n.p.

[3]George Balanchine, "The Dance Element in Stravinsky's Music," *Stravinsky in the Theatre*, ed. Minna Lederman (New York: Da Capo, 1949) 81.

[4]Robert Garis, in his article "Balanchine – Stravinsky: Facts and Problems" (*Ballet Review* 10.3, Fall 1982, 9-23), argues that the Stravinsky-Balanchine partnership was never as egalitarian as later chroniclers portrayed it, and that Balanchine himself harbored certain

choreographer admits that his first collaboration with Stravinsky was a revelation for him:

> It was in studying *Apollon* that I came first to understand how gestures, like tones in music and shades in painting, have certain family relations... Since this work, I have developed my choreography inside the framework such relations suggest.[5]

Like Stravinsky's compositions, Balanchine's works reveal a cosmopolitan and variegated cultural aesthetic and a willingness to borrow, transform, or co-exist with widely disparate elements of Western and non-Western culture, be they literary, popular, or religious. Both men embraced their adoptive cultures willingly without abandoning their Russian roots. Stravinsky's magpie-like curiosity took him far afield, from Classical verse forms such as the Alexandrine to Slavic folk fables, to text sources as varied as the Catholic liturgy and the writings of W. H. Auden. Balanchine, while less consciously and rigorously intellectual, felt comfortable using images of the American West, Classical mythology, even pop culture. Both men worked within, rather than outside, their adoptive cultures, and the synthesis of tradition and innovation is a salient feature of their work.

Stravinsky was fortunate to have been born into a society, a city, and a social echelon which was then at its culmination: the bourgeois upper class aristocracy of late nineteenth-century St. Petersburg. Long considered the Russian gateway to Europe, St. Petersburg enjoyed a centuries-old reputation as a cosmopolitan and sophisticated city where the Russian and European cultural worlds were artfully combined. Russia's greatest ensembles and schools could be found there: the Alexandrinsky Theatre, center of Russian dramatic arts; the Imperial Opera, where the composer's father performed as a basso; and the famous Maryinsky Theater, where the works of the country's great nineteenth-century Nationalist composers were performed. Stravinsky

---

unexpressed misgivings about Stravinsky's creative dominance, his opinions of choreography in general, even his music. Garis' suppositions, while well-reasoned, are based on circumstantial evidence and critical observations only, and are largely contradicted by numerous respected firsthand observers of the Stravinsky-Balanchine partnership such as Vera Stravinsky, Violette Verdy and Olga Maynard.

[5]Balanchine 81-82.

studied in St. Petersburg with the undisputed late-nineteenth-century inheritor of that Nationalist tradition, the composer Nicolas Rimsky-Korsakov.

Balanchine enjoyed similar cultural privileges, although his family was by no means rich. His father was a composer and arranger of traditional folk songs of the Caucasus. Balanchine was accepted at an early age into the Imperial School of Theatre and Ballet at the Maryinsky Theatre; state subsidies assured students a superlative education with the nation's greatest artists.

In addition to ballet and theatre studies, his wide-ranging education included rigorous schooling in music. This solid grounding in an art so integral to choreography is, sadly and ironically, a rather rare attribute among twentieth-century choreographers, and it was one of Balanchine's most valuable educational assets. Like his father, Balanchine was a promising if not masterful composer, and he studied briefly with Glazunov at the Leningrad Conservatory. He was an accomplished pianist, and a capable amateur conductor.[6] His approach to choreography was intrinsically musical: "Balanchine thought of himself as a musician, and of his choreography as a musical operation – a making visible in movement what he heard in a piece of music."[7] Balanchine subjected each score on which he worked to rigorous analysis, often amazing others with his intimate understanding of the music at hand.[8]

Despite the fact that Russia was a much less stable country during his own youth than during Stravinsky's, Balanchine was fortunate to have been largely spared the vicissitudes of the First World War (though not the devastating years of the Russian Revolution). His education was relatively

---

[6]Violette Verdy, interview with Gretchen Jacobson, 16 October 1986 (unpublished: University of California, Irvine library), 162. See also Robert Craft, ed., *Stravinsky: Selected Correspondence*, v. 1, 340, 340n.

[7]B. H. Haggin, "Reflections on Balanchine," *Dance Magazine* (July 1983): 56.

[8]Alexandra Danilova, "Danilova on Balanchine," *Dance Magazine* (July 1983): 62. See also Bernard Taper, *Balanchine: A Biography* (1960; New York: Macmillan, 1974) 55-56.

unimpeded during a period of great social upheaval, and he graduated from the ballet school of the Alexandrinsky Theatre in 1921.

Their common origins imbued both men with similar artistic sensibilities. Both adhered to the rather quaintly old-fashioned concept of the creative artist as a craftsman, working willingly with available resources and under specific and accepted practical restrictions resulting from the inevitable considerations of budget, targeted audience and the like. They did not subscribe to the popular Romantic conceit of the artist as a capricious and inspiration-driven genius who worked alone, answering only to his own inviolable vision.

Advised Stravinsky to his young collaborator during the making of *Apollon:* "Be precise, imaginative, formal – never attempt to create a masterpiece, only a well made work of art."[9]   Indeed, the concept of restrictiveness, whether external or self-imposed, was a crucial one, especially to Stravinsky. In his *Poetics of Music* he states: "when variety tempts me, I am uneasy about the facile solutions it offers me. Similarity, on the other hand, poses more difficult problems but also offers results that are more solid and hence more valuable to me."[10]

Balanchine's choreography, too, flourished under the ostensible dictates of Apollonian/Stravinskian restraint. In later works such as *Agon*, the movement vocabulary has been pared down to its most elegantly fundamental form; adornments and mannerisms are banished; the keen and hypnotic power of choreomusical affinity is laid bare. This choreographic clarity allows us to observe and understand music-movement relationships of tremendous complexity, such as densely contrapuntal textures. Moreover we can see, in these ballets particularly, that one of Balanchine's aesthetic *raisons d'être* was the often precise (but never obvious) realization of the processes of music in movement, and that this relationship is often multi-layered, pervasive and subtle.

---

[9]Baird Hastings, *Choreographer and Composer* (Boston: Twayne Publishers, 1983) 128-129.

[10]Igor Stravinsky, *Poetics of Music* (Cambridge: Harvard University Press, 1970) 54.

Concerning the exact nature of the collaborative process between Stravinsky and Balanchine, little accurate or complete information has been written. During the conception of later works such as *Orpheus* and *Agon*, the two men enjoyed the luxury of greater time for the conceptual process. Vera Stravinsky claims that during the genesis of *Agon* they would frequently work, sequestered in Stravinsky's California studio, for an entire day. "Each time they came out [they] were very satisfied. [Stravinsky] would say, 'Good, we did a lot today.'"[11] Vera Stravinsky adds, too, that Balanchine occasionally sent Stravinsky's music back to him with requests for changes; indeed, Balanchine was one of the only people for whom Stravinsky was willing to have provided them. Of course, the opposite was also true. During one famous rehearsal of *Agon*, Stravinsky made several choreographic suggestions which were incorporated by Balanchine into the work.[12] After a lifelong relationship with the ballet, Stravinsky had become a keen and informed observer of dance movement:

> [Stravinsky's] is the profound stage instinct of an amateur of
> the dance, the "amateur" whose attitude is so professional that
> it seems merely an accident that he is not himself a dancer.[13]

From a lifetime of close professional collaboration, then, let us examine three works which are generally acknowledged as masterpieces in the repertoires of both Igor Stravinsky and George Balanchine and uncover the relationships between score and choreography which help to make them remarkable.

---

[11] Vera Stravinsky 6.

[12] See photo montage with accompanying description in Taper 269-276.

[13] Lincoln Kirstein, "Working With Stravinsky," *Stravinsky in the Theatre*, ed. Minna Lederman (New York: Da Capo, 1949) 137.

APOLLON MUSAGÈTE

Choreography by George Balanchine

Score by Igor Stravinsky

There is ample evidence that *Apollon Musagète* was regarded by both Igor Stravinsky and George Balanchine as a significant and even seminal work. To the young choreographer, the opportunity of working with Stravinsky was a dream come true, the culmination of years of admiration, even veneration, of the composer's work. Balanchine had earlier choreographed to Stravinsky scores such as *Pulcinella* and *Rossignol*; by the age of 24 he was thoroughly familiar with the composer's style – he reportedly owned every Stravinsky score that was then available in Russia.[1] To Balanchine, *Apollon* represented a landmark of sorts, and its creation was a self-described epiphanic event in his creative development:

> *Apollon* I look back on as the turning point in my life. In its discipline and restraint, in its sustained oneness of tone and feeling the score was a revelation. It seemed to tell me that I could dare not to use everything, that I, too, could eliminate...
>
> I examined my own work in light of this lesson. I began to see how I could clarify, by limiting, by reducing what seemed to be multiple possibilities to the one that is inevitable.[2]

---

[1] Nancy Lassalle, ed., "Stravinsky and Balanchine: Fifty Years of Partnership: 1920-1971" (New York: New York City Ballet, 1971) n.p.

[2] George Balanchine, "The Dance Element in Stravinsky's Music," *Stravinsky in the Theatre*, ed. Minna Ledermann (New York: Da Capo, 1949) 81.

Balanchine particularly admired Stravinsky's predilection for precision and exact definition of intent. He was once chastised by the composer for not knowing the exact length of a section to be choreographed. Noted Balanchine:

> Stravinsky, as a collaborator, breaks down every task to essentials. He thinks first, and sometimes last, of time duration – how much is needed for the introduction, the pas de deux, the variations, the coda. To have all the time in the world means nothing to him.[3]

Not surprisingly, these qualities, often referred to by Stravinsky himself as "Apollonian," begin to appear too in Balanchine's work from this point forward.

Balanchine was not the original choreographer of *Apollon.* It received its premiere on April 27, 1928, at the Library of Congress in Washington, D.C., with choreography by Adolph Bolm. But Stravinsky, who could be notoriously caustic toward choreographers who, in his opinion, did not successfully interpret his music (one has only to read his disparaging comments about Nijinsky to appreciate this quality), much preferred the Balanchine version; he later remarked that "the success of *Apollo* must be attributed...to the beauty of Balanchine's choreography."[4] He professed himself altogether satisfied with the skillfulness of Balanchine's use of the score, especially at the beginning and in the "troika" section of the Coda.[5]

Curiously, the satisfaction of both choreographer and composer at the work's premiere was not widely reflected in the comments of the critics. Though by no means condemnatory, initial critical reaction was only mildly supportive and occasionally even negative. Of its London premiere, the *Times* critic wrote: "It used to be said that the Russian Ballet would not be much without Stravinsky: his latest production makes us fear that soon it will

---

[3]Balanchine 84.

[4]Igor Stravinsky and Robert Craft, *Dialogues and a Diary* (Garden City: Doubleday, 1963) 18.

[5]Stravinsky and Craft 18.

not be much with him."[6] The composer also claims to have been hurt by dismissive comments concerning the score. French and English critics, it seems, heard all manner of banal references to other music – a characteristic of the score which Stravinsky claims was completely unintentional.[7] Critic Gordon Craig, though, was so moved by the performance that he left the concert hall immediately after seeing it, missing the rest of the program, and he rightly claimed it a musical and choreographic masterpiece.

Clearly, Stravinsky was pleased with the score itself; he saw fit to record and conduct it in concert many times over the next forty years.[8] Balanchine, too, revived the work a number of times, and it was subjected to several revisions: the initial scene depicting the birth of Apollo was eventually deleted, the number of performers reduced to just four, the costumes and sets simplified, and the final Apotheosis altered. Despite the relative coolness of its initial reception, *Apollon Musagète* has been elevated to a place of unique importance in Balanchine's *oeuvre*, and it is now widely considered to be his first "milestone" choreography, a work which crystallized and defined his aesthetic and established a standard of achievement which he was to maintain for years to come. Edwin Denby describes the significance of Balanchine's achievement in *Apollo* this way:

> Extraordinary is the richness with which he can, with only four dancers, create a sustained and more and more satisfying impression of man's creative genius, depicting it concretely in its grace, its sweet wit, its force and boldness, and with the constant warmth of its sensuous complicity with physical beauty...it leaves at the end, despite its innumerable incidental inventions, a sense of bold, open, effortless and limpid grandeur.[9]

---

[6]Richard Buckle and John Taras, *George Balanchine: Ballet Master* (London: Hamish Hamilton Ltd., 1988) 46-47.

[7]Stravinsky and Craft 18.

[8]For a detailed account of *Apollon's* many performances, refer to Robert Craft, ed., *Stravinsky: Selected Correspondence*, v. 1, 2 (New York: Alfred A. Knopf, 1982).

[9]Bernard Taper, *Balanchine* (New York: Macmillan, 1974) 104.

Stravinsky, too, felt that *Apollon* ushered forth a new personal stylistic period, one which had pervasive and long-lasting effects:

> *Apollo* was my largest single step toward a long-line polyphonic style, and though it has a harmonic and melodic, above all an intervallic, character of its own, it nourished many later works as well.[10]

He was especially excited by the opportunity *Apollon* afforded him to write music which was highly melodic in nature – a lost craft, Stravinsky thought, in the atmosphere of dissonance and "newness for newness' sake" which permeated the European compositional aesthetic of the time:

> The taste for melody *per se* having been lost, it was no longer cultivated for its own sake, and there was therefore no criterion by which its value could be assessed. It seemed to me that it was not only timely but urgent to turn once more to the cultivation of this element from a purely musical point of view.[11]

Extrinsic choreomusical relationships in *Apollon* emanate primarily from the narrative source itself, the mythological story of the life of the god Apollo. Perhaps the most pervasive extrinsic musical reference is the conscious imitation of the Alexandrine, a type of French heroic verse whose name is derived from the twelfth- and thirteenth-century poems relating the life of Alexander the Great. The musical introduction, "Naissance d'Apollon," introduces us to a dotted eighth-sixteenth-note figure which approximates the cadence of this form of iambic verse.

---

[10]Stravinsky and Craft 19.

[11]Igor Stravinsky, "Stravinsky's Own Story," Lederman 158.

NAISSANCE D'APOLLON

Figure 1: mm. 1-3

The patterns of iambic stress were intended to be almost constantly apparent throughout the score.[12] Although Stravinsky makes no attempt to adhere continually to the classic Alexandrine line length of six iambic feet (such a conceit would have been too restrictive even for him), the literary reference is nonetheless appropriate: Apollo's life has been celebrated in verse since the Homeric poems of ancient times. Stravinsky's poetic references are often quite contemporary, however. At certain moments the score even refers to specific Alexandrines from Russian and French literary sources such as Pushkin and Boileau.[13]

The choice of a string orchestra with its limited timbral possibilities is, of course, also a clever extrinsic reference. Strings are the embodiment of the Apollonian ethos of calmness and restraint, light and goodness, an iconographic association which may be traced to Classical sources and which became especially apparent in Renaissance depictions of Classical mythology. It was the logical orchestrational choice for Apollo, long known as

---

[12]See Stravinsky and Craft 17.

[13]Stravinsky and Craft 17-18.

the god of light (later identified with Helios the Sun) and so of inspiration, which does for the soul what light does for the world: swift and powerful as the sun's rays, he was the dazzlingly splendid young Lord of music and song.[14]

The lyre, of course, has long been associated with music-making among Gods and mythological heroes; it is a feature of both the Apollonian and Orphic legends. "The lyre and the curved bow shall ever be dear to me," declares the infant Apollo, and both string and bow find their appropriate musical evocation in the form of the string orchestra.[15]

Self-imposed compositional and orchestrational constraints are a characteristic Stravinsky technique as well, particularly in this relatively early stage of his Neoclassical period. In *Apollon* he attempted to compose a score "in which contrasts of volumes replace contrasts of instrumental colors."[16] The composer chose a highly limited palette of motive and color possibilities, leaving dynamic variation and changes of tessitura as the principal means of contrast. In his attempt to evoke the purity of line associated with "white ballet," Stravinsky sought a musical medium of similar quality. With a string orchestra,

> I found that the absence of many-colored effects and of all superfluities produced a wonderful freshness. This inspired me to write music of an analagous character. It seemed to me that diatonic composition was the most appropriate for this purpose, and the austerity of its style determined what my instrumental ensemble must be. I at once set aside the ordinary orchestra because of its heterogeneity...and I chose strings...[17]

Balanchine's movement language also exhibits a Neoclassical restraint and a deliberately restrictive vocabulary. In its final revised form, the work is intimate in scale and requires only four dancers: Apollo and the three Muses. Each of the Muses is consigned a specific and highly prescriptive set of movement patterns, all quite stylized and concentrated. Each dancer reflects

---

[14]Michael Grant, *Myths of the Greeks and Romans* (New York: Mentor, 1962) 121.

[15]Grant 119.

[16]Stravinsky and Craft 19.

[17]Stravinsky 158.

the characteristics of her mythological archetype in consice, economical, ways. There is no wasted motion.

These choreographic and musical choices, within a narrative context, obviously set the stage for instances of mimetic and archetypal conceit. Indeed, among the choreomusical relationships found in *Apollon,* these predominate, and their repetition forms the thematic schema of the work, defining its event-based temporal structure. Other relationships, while by no means infrequent, are usually integral components of these more substantive correspondences.

*   *   *   *   *

The sources to which I refer are, for the score, the revised edition (Boosey & Hawkes, 1947) and, for the choreography, the version presented in the 1982 PBS broadcast of the New York City Ballet's Stravinsky Festival Concerts from the Lincoln Center.

In this final version of the work, Balanchine has chosen to eliminate the introductory action, during which Leto gives birth to Apollo and he is unwrapped from his swaddling clothes.[18] By virtue of this elimination, the choreographer highlights Apollo's first strong movement statement: the striking of the lyre at rehearsal 20 in the score.

Fig. 2: R. 20 – R.21

---

[18]Balanchine's numerous revisions of *Apollon* have met with some criticism. Robert Garis (in "Balanchine-Stravinsky: Facts and Problems" [*Ballet Review* 10.3, Fall 1982]) argues that such editing destroys important elements of symmetry in both story and score, and many important thematic relationships suffer as a result.

It is here that the first overt example of mimetic conceit occurs. Apollo's lyre playing is represented by a brilliant and athletic violin solo. It contains obvious dynamic, rhythmic and textural relationships, all serving to strengthen the extrinsic affinity of Apollo's mimed lute playing. But choreographer and composer do not attempt to achieve literal mimetic action. Instead of merely imitating the idiomatic characteristics of the lyre, the violin solo captures the essence of Apollo's loose-limbed athleticism in a series of alternating trills and sweeping sixteenth and thirty-second note figures. Apollo's "playing" movements are carefully coordinated to the cadences and trills of the violin line. His swinging arm, gradually accelerating in speed, corresponds to the increasing rapidity of the solo into R. 21. Thus we see a relationship that functions on two levels: the music offers a direct (if highly stylized) imitation of the lyre; as an archetypal conceit, though, the violin solo and Apollo's movement quality both comment more subtly on the nature of his personality and intent.

At R. 21 we hear a pronounced iambic rhythm in the two solo violin lines, accompanied by a regular *pizzicato* rhythm in the lower strings.

Fig. 3: R. 21–21 + 12

Fig. 3, *continued*

The clear antecedent-consequent relationship between the two violin phrases (R. 21 and R. 21 + 8) is accompanied by a clear structural parallel in the movement. Apollo's reaching *relevé* phrase is performed twice, each time in a different direction and with a different facing: the first upstage right diagonally and backward, the second downstage left diagonally and forward. As would be expected, the dance and music phrases correspond temporally.

Textural parallels may be observed at R. 31 + 3. The lower strings deliver a *forte* line marked *en dehors* and *marcato espressivo*. The upper strings play a more active rhythmic counterpoint marked *pianissimo subito*. Apollo's movements assume the character of the lower line: precise, muscular, and kinetic. The Muses act as one dancer, moving in unison, just as the upper strings play in homophony. The relationship between choreographic and musical counterpoint is obvious. The opposing musical textures begin to meld after R. 32; so too does the stylistic separation between Apollo's movements and those of the Muses. Balanchine here shows a keen sensitivity to changing musical texture.

Fig. 4: R. 31 + 3 − R. 33

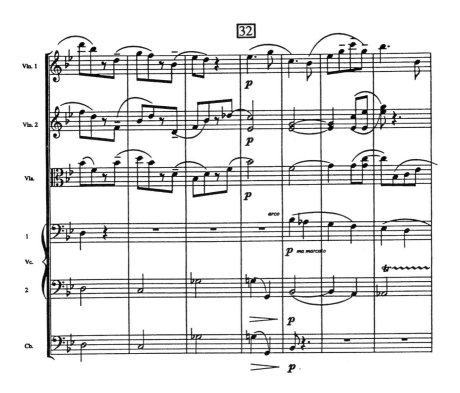

Fig. 4, *continued*

Fig. 4, *continued*

Apollo arranges the Muses

Photo: Paul Kolnik

Balanchine uses the technique of textural contrast to amusing results at the end of the "Variation de Polymnie" (Polymnie was the Goddess of Poetry). Here the choreographer effects a humorous inversion of audience expectations. In the last measures (R. 51 + 10) a loud *pizzicato* chord is used to emphasize a mimed shout by the dancer. This is followed immediately by a bowed chord, to which Polymnie quickly contracts, taking back her forbidden spoken word. We would expect just the opposite musical setting for this choreographic effect: the penultimate chord *arco,* the final chord *pizzicato.* Instead, the music fortifies the amusing absurdity of the movement's implication through unexpected contrast.

Fig. 5: R. 51 + 10

At R. 34 we see an example of a textural contrast which contains a subtle connective relationship. The Muses perform small skips onto *pointe* which at first seem deliberately ignored in the prevailingly smooth *cantabile* musical lines. But after several viewings, it becomes apparent that the short, repeated rhythmic burst in violin II bears more than a passing relationship to the movement.

Fig. 6: R. 34 + 1–4

A more noticeable example of qualitative and dynamic contrast occurs at the end of "Variation d'Apollon" (R. 63 + 5-7). To homorhythmic, strident music marked *fortissimo* and *poco a poco rallentando,* Apollo sinks first to his knees, then to the floor, and as Terpsichore enters from downstage right to touch his hand, they look away from each other as the strings cadence strongly. A deliberate contrast of musical and choreographic quality and dynamic is achieved.

The most striking example of archetypal conceit is the famous "troika" section (as Stravinsky charmingly refers to it), from R. 89 to R. 93. Apollo leads the three Muses as though they are horses pulling him in a chariot. The music, a repeated section in 2/4 time marked *cantabile,* has a scherzo quality with simple, folk-like melodies in the first violins and first cellos. The musical and choreographic effect is muscular, crude and evocative of equestrian movement, with ascending *marcato* quarter notes in the lower strings and a pervasive repeated rhythmic cell in the violas.

Fig. 7: R. 89-R. 90 + 4

Fig. 7, *continued*

There are, of course, many other easily categorizable music-to-movement relationships in *Apollon Musagète*. Some, however, are tremendously subtle and require more detailed and less categorical analysis than the paradigm allows.

One such event occurs four measures before R. 41. As the melody in violin I ascends, Calliope runs quickly downstage. She leaps as the melody reaches its apex, and she lands at the beginning of the next musical phrase, the anacrusis to the following measure (in violin II). The phrase group disintegrates neatly into two-note slurs as her leaps become successively smaller. Here Balanchine has used the dancer in a quasi-instrumental way to join by movement two related phrases in the score.

At the beginning of "Variation d'Apollon" the music becomes noticeably stronger and more kinetic. The homorhythmic opening chords are closely allied to Apollo's strident arm movements. Balanchine uses the ascending *pizzicato* cello motive as the impetus for a repeated *jeté* pattern. But this motive, while it initially supports the jumps, soon falls out of step with the movement. The notes are conscious augmentations of the more compact movement motive. This represents a contrast to the close hands-to-music correlation occurring simultaneously. Slowly the music transforms itself to become the dynamic equal of the movement, culminating in the "cadential" motive which accompanies the return to the original swinging arm movement and jump at R. 61.

Fig. 8: R. 61

After this point, however, there is the curious, pervasive feeling that the music is generally under-supportive of the strident choreography, although some intrinsic music-movement relationships remain quite overt (for example, the rhythmic and qualitative relationships between the leg movements and the ascending sixteenth note *pizzicato* motive in the cellos at R. 62). By the final cadence of the movement the situation has been reversed. The music has become *fortissimo* and strident, and the movement is relatively weak dynamically. Thus Apollo's seeming strength is continually undermined and finally defeated by the music, which assumes in its final form a fragmentary resemblance to the violin theme in the following *pas de deux* (at R. 66).

There are, of course, countless other fascinating examples of choreomusical relationship in *Apollon Musagète*, yet even an analysis of this modest scope reveals the degree to which Stravinsky and Balanchine have expressed the Apollonian ethos. "Know thyself, his priests taught – understand your station as man and do not overstep it; bow before the divine."[19] He was, after all, the god empowered with the approval of codes of conduct, and his laws were intended to encourage high moral and religious principles. He was the god of calmness and order. In depicting the Apollonian myth, choreographer and composer have captured his spirit as well, and the work reverberates with the magic of exquisitely crafted choreomusical effects which help to achieve this end. More fascinating, though, are the subtlety of those effects. Balanchine almost continually avoids or inverts the obvious choreomusical affinities, encouraging us to look for deeper and more significant family relationships, and joining each choreomusical event into this underlying framework.

---

[19]Grant 122.

Photo: Paul Kolnik

Tableau freeze

ORPHEUS

Choreography by George Balanchine

Score by Igor Stravinsky

The care and time lavished on *Orpheus* by both Stravinsky and Balanchine are well-documented.[1] Both men took a strong interest in many different aspects of the production. They frequently visited the studio of sculptor Isamu Noguchi, for example, to check on the progress of the ballet's immense sets. Stravinsky arrived in New York City a full three weeks before the scheduled premiere of April 28, 1948, and he attended nearly all the dance rehearsals.[2]

The elements of restraint, compactness, and emotional understatement which Stravinsky demonstrated and Balanchine discovered in *Apollon* – the salient characteristics of Neoclassicism – run like a common thread through the mature works of both men, reaching their culmination in *Orpheus* and, in a later, more highly distilled form, *Agon*. Although Balanchine utilized a larger *corp de ballet* here than in the spartan *Apollon*, Stravinsky limited himself to a comparatively small instrumental ensemble: woodwinds in pairs, four horns, two trumpets, two trombones, timpani, harp, and a small string section.

---

[1]Fascinating and detailed evidence of the ballet's production process can be found in *Stravinsky: Selected Correspondence*, ed. Robert Craft, v. 1 (New York: Knopf, 1982) 265-71.

[2]Bernard Taper, *Balanchine: A Biography* (New York: Macmillan, 1974) 234-237.

Any musical treatment of the Orpheus legend begs comparison with previous attempts, and of the two most famous settings, Stravinsky's version bears a more striking resemblance to Monteverdi's than to Gluck's.[3] Indeed, his score is in many ways an homage. Just as *The Rake's Progress* isolates and redefines elements of musical Classicism, *Orpheus* utilizes late Renaissance and early Baroque stylistic conventions. The use of the descending Phrygian scale in the opening harp motive is historically evocative, both in its acknowledgement of the mode's emotional implications and in the obvious "madrigalism" of narrative foreshadowing in the melodic contour. This short, repeated phrase becomes an important (though sparingly used) motive later in the work, as we shall see.

Stravinsky could not have been unaware of the common Renaissance conceits concerning instrumental affects, nor of the manner in which Monteverdi used them. Renaissance art frequently brings these conceits into full focus: the depiction of woodwind instruments, for example, as representative of the pastoral world, the bucolic libertine sphere of aristocratic fantasy; or, in more extreme cases, the opposition of stringed instruments and woodwinds as symbols of good and evil respectively.[4] The lyre, long associated with Orphic legend, was the instrument Orpheus used to accompany his own bewitching songs, and is frequently associated with divine or mythological music-making in Renaissance art.[5]

---

[3] Igor Stravinsky, *Orpheus* (London: Boosey & Hawkes, 1948).

[4] Two well-known examples are Correggio's "Allegory of Vice" and "Allegory of Virtue" (ca. 1531, Musée du Louvre, Paris). In the former, an obviously excited Vice is being enticed by a recorder-playing nymph. In the latter, a "virtuous" maid is surrounded by seraphim-like attendants, including a lutenist. The intent of the paintings was clearly moralistic and didactic, and the implied symbolism of the instruments needed no further explication. In Lorenzo da Costa's "An Allegory Painted for Isabella d'Este's *Studiolo*" (1504-06, Musée du Louvre, Paris) we see a more forceful example of allgorical imagery. In the midst of a veritable ocean of violence, brutality and vice lies a garden of tranquillity where a queen, surrounded by musicians and artists, is about to be crowned. All four musicians play stringed instruments.

[5] In Mantegna's "Parnassus" (undated, Musée du Louvre, Paris) Mercury and Apollo stand side by side. Apollo plays the lyre, which was invented by Mercury. In the center foreground are the nine Muses; some are singing, all are dancing.

In Monteverdi's *L'Orfeo* (1608) these allusions are frequently made plain in a score which is unusual for the time in its richness of orchestration. In the third act, for example, as Orfeo crosses the River Styx, the score calls for trombones, cornets, and *organi di legno* to accompany his solo, creating an appropriately dark and ominous effect.[6] Later in the act, under Caronte's solo, the accompaniment is scored for *regale*, a nasal reed organ of unusual timbre. Afterwards, there is a contrapuntal duet for cornets, further reinforcing the association of woodwinds, soft brass and reedy organ with scenes concerning the underworld. The harp is often employed under Orfeo's arias in imitation of the lyre.

Stravinsky's orchestration, while not overtly similar to Monteverdi's in its treatment of instrumental affects, does bear striking affinities in some crucial respects. Both composers use instruments of low, dark timbre and highlight their low and middle tessituras, especially in scenes which deal with Hades. In Stravinsky's score a low trombone solo at R. 36 accompanies Orpheus' descent into Tartarus (Hades), and the "Pas des Furies" is filled with sections for low woodwinds and brass. The frequent appearance of paired bassoons (in the first "Air de Danse," for example) could be seen as an oblique reference to Monteverdi's use of the similar-sounding *regale*, and the contrapuntal duet for horns in the Apotheosis (R. 143) is reminiscent of the instrumental duets in Act 3 of *L'Orfeo*. Most striking, of course, is the concertante use of the harp, the modern equivalent of the characteristic Orphic instrument, in both works.

In *Orpheus*, Stravinsky and Balanchine are careful to set their prevailing emotional and compositional tone at the outset. The first scene is one of bereavement. Orpheus stands with his back to the audience, weeping for Eurydice at her graveside. The music is simple, with a slow harmonic rhythm; the harp is established as the voice of his instrument, the lyre. The score is gentle and unobtrusive as friends arrive, bearing gifts and offering sympathy. The delicacy of the musical setting, the coolness of Balanchine's

---

[6]Claudio Monteverdi, *L'Orfeo* , ed. G. Francesco Malipiero (London: J. & W. Chester, Ltd., 1923).

64

group tableaux and his studied use of asymmetry act as portals through which we gently pass as we are drawn into the action of the story.

As the work unfolds, it becomes clear that the two artists have chosen to approach the story differently. Balanchine treats it in the manner of an episodic narrative, with each scene following logically on the last. In the score, however, no such obvious connection between movements is attempted, although certain material is repeated. Thus a curious choreomusical tension is created in the contrasting approach to extrinsic relationships, Balanchine using extrinsic referents in a more direct and linear fashion, Stravinsky developing more oblique extrinsic references.

At rehearsal number 7 in the score, Orpheus builds an effigy of Eurydice, using his lyre and the gifts he has received as the elements of its construction. The score at this point contains a covered line for low trombone, an intervallically similar augmentation of the initial harp motive – like the descending harp line, another example of narrative foreshadowing.

Fig. 1: R. 7 - R. 8

This is the first of many instances of the orchestrational association of low, dark instrumental timbres with the underworld – a clear archetypal relationship in the music. While no strong intrinsic choreomusical relationship exists at this point, the music does echo the soft, rounded gestures of Orpheus' lamentation in gentle rhythmic parallel.

At R. 12, repeated harp chords marked *étouffé marcato* are heard as Orpheus strokes his lyre, the first of numerous examples of mimetic conceit concerning his instrument. Stravinsky himself claimed that "...much of *Orpheus* is mimed song."[7]

---

[7]Igor Stravinsky, *Themes and Conclusions* (London: Faber and Faber, 1972) 53.

Fig. 2: R. 12 - R. 12 + 3

As in *Apollon*, exact imitation is never the object of either choreographer or composer. Here the strings accompany the harp in a rhythmic underlay of repeated notes. This string accompaniment itself becomes an important thematic element later in the scene, at R. 13 and R. 16-2, in two of the most sunny and joyous moments of the score. Yet the motive has no obvious immediate movement parallel. Stravinsky may be alluding here to the emotional effect of Orpheus' singing and playing, which reportedly "brought joy and pleasure to all who heard (him)."[8]

An interesting knot of textural, rhythmic and dynamic parallels can be seen after the *corp* enters at R. 13. In the score the two bassoons share melodically and rhythmically similar but not identical lines, as do the horn and cellos. All four instrumental voices together form an unbroken but texturally heterogeneous line until the second entry of the upper string motive at R. 15 + 2.

---

[8]Stanley Sadie, ed., *The New Grove Dictionary of Music and Musicians*, v. 13 (London: Macmillan, 1980) 870-871.

66

Fig. 3: R. 13 + 1 - R. 15

In the same fashion, the line of dancers which has formed upstage executes movements on *pointe* which are similar in dynamic but not identical. Just as the dancers constitute an unbroken but internally varied horizontal line, so do the melodic lines of the bassoons, horn and cellos, while individually short-breathed, in concert create a long, unbroken phrase. The movement phrase, while heterogeneous, maintains a constant eighth-note rhythm, imitating perfectly the cello "pulse" from R. 13 + 3 through R. 15 + 2.

From R. 21 to R. 24 the first measures of the "Air de Danse" are essentially repeated as Orpheus returns to the effigy of Eurydice. The repetition of the rising bassoon and flute motive at this point, as Orpheus visibly yearns for his departed lover, firmly establishes the woodwinds, particularly the low-timbred bassoons, as the imploring voice of the underworld calling up to Orpheus (notice, too, that the clarinets are in *chalumeau* register). Thus the archetypal and narrative relationships are reinforced: the low, rising instrumental line serves as a call from the underworld, triggering a choreographic "answer" from Orpheus.

68

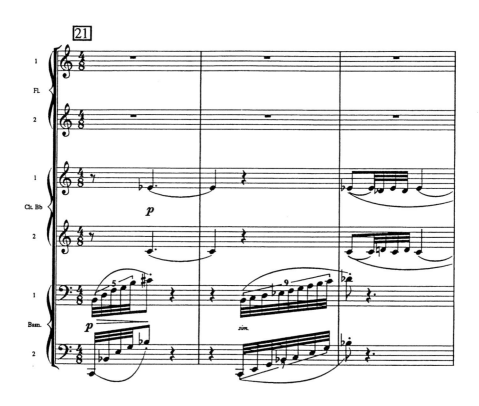

Fig. 4: R. 21-24

From R. 22 to R. 27 Orpheus dances around the lyre-effigy as the strings continue to expand on the ostinato motive which was so firmly associated with his lyre-playing at R. 12 + 2.

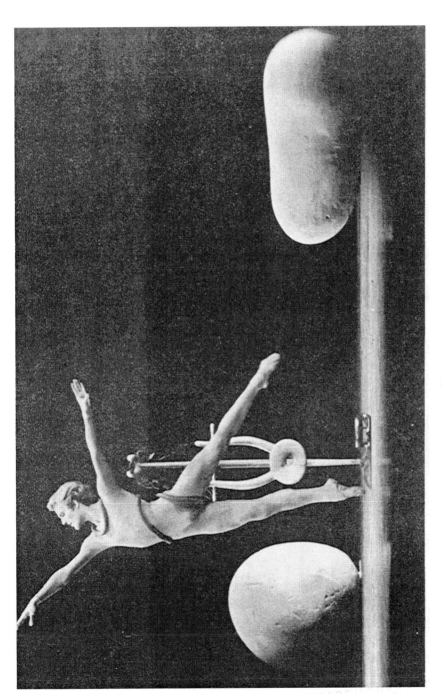

Orpheus dances around the lyre-effigy

Photo: Paul Kolnik

As Orpheus strums his lyre at R. 22, a triadic clarinet line provides the lyre "sound" in the score.

Fig. 5: R. 22

This mimetic conceit is a marked contrast to the original instance with harp, and our sensibilities are subtly piqued with a timbral surprise. At R. 26 the dry contrabass line provides additional foreshadowing as it presents an augmented and roughly inverted fragment of the harp's signature motive. The scene ends as it had begun, with a rising woodwind line (this time in the flutes) appearing as a taunting and distant call, imploring Orpheus from afar.

Fig. 6: R. 27 + 1 - 3

At both R. 17 and R. 24 the score provides an unsettling, insistent sixteenth-note triplet figure as Orpheus appears to search for Eurydice, or at least an entranceway to Tartarus. As the tableau ends the viewer is left with the impression that the motive in the upper strings at R. 13 and R. 16 has acted as a call or a summons to action, galvanizing Orpheus on its second appearance to agitation and resolve.

In the next section, the "Dance of the Angel of Death," the prominent instruments are low strings, low woodwinds, and horns, all playing subdued dynamics of mf or below. The generally low, dark tessituras and soft dynamics throughout this scene create both narrative and archetypal associations. Instead of establishing a characteristic motive or instrument with the Angel, Stravinsky instead provides a characteristic timbral color, register and dynamic level. The effect is particularly noticeable beginning at R. 34. As the Angel prepares to lead Orpheus to Tartarus, several measures of very low, quiet held chords are heard in the lower woodwinds, followed by a descending harp line.

Fig. 7: R. 34 to R. 40

From R. 36 to R. 40, as Orpheus and the Angel descend, Stravinsky presents a meandering trombone solo with a chilling tremolo string accompaniment.

Fig. 8: R. 36 - R. 40 + 4

74

Fig. 8, *continued*

This archetypal conceit is one of several instances in which the trombone specifically is imbued with connotations of the underworld.[9]

As Orpheus and the Angel arrive in the gloom of Tartarus, the two horns quietly imitate the beginning of the trombone's earlier solo, repeating it several times with a softly accented insistence and adding a momentary textural parallel to the end of the duet.

The movement quality in the duet during the Interlude is appropriately slow, deliberate, and sinuous. Movements occur only every two or four quarter note beats–slower even than the music's harmonic rhythm.

The "Pas des Furies" begins with a low horn motive at R. 47 + 3–6, further emphasizing the association of low brass timbres with the underworld.

---

[9]By the late eigtheenth century, the trombone had developed strong associations with the ecclesiastical or supernatural. Gluck used a trombone trio for the oracle scene in *Alceste*. Mozart used the trombone only in religious works and operas–the supper scene in *Don Giovanni* is one of the most famous operatic examples of the trombone's supernatural affiliations; and trombones are found in the *tuba mirum* of his Requiem Mass.

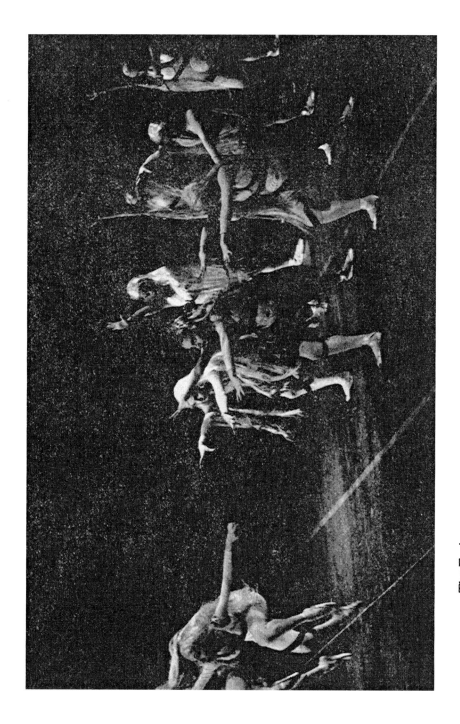

Photo: Martha Swope

The Furies

Fig. 9: R. 47 + 3 - + 6

Nervous string figures and quick flute arpeggios are paired with the rapid, agitated running movements of the Furies. A textural parallel can be observed in this section between the number of Furies onstage and the number of independent musical lines in the score. Even here, in the midst of a marked increase in the choreographic energy level, Stravinsky keeps a comparatively tight rein on his constructive rules: tessituras remain prevailingly low (with some exceptions in the woodwinds), and the dynamics peak at mf. The trumpet motive at R. 58 announces the stirring of a second group of Furies. The score is repeated from R. 50 to R. 61, the second time with all Furies active. The trombones sneak in after R. 60, trombone 2 delivering a sparse variation of the original descending harp motive at R. 62.

Fig. 10: R. 62 and adjacent bars

At R. 63 the repeated-note figure, a secondary element of the preceding section, becomes more insistent in a new tempo marked *Sempre alla breve ma meno mosso*. Accordingly, the movement of the Furies becomes more insistent, in a clear example of rhythmic parallel. In this section two thematic parallels also become established:

1) the *perpetuum mobile* eighth-note pattern, now transformed into a more blatant motor rhythm, is the Furies' running impetus.

2) the rhythmic motive, beginning with a dotted eighth-rest, which figures prominently in violin I and viola from R. 63 to R. 71, corresponds to a wild "flying up" arm motion in the Furies' choreography.

Fig. 11: R. 63 1 - 4

Also in this section, Stravinsky has carefully orchestrated a slowly rising, then falling phrase in the strings to give a sense of progression and completion to a dance which contains little linear development or climax by itself. The choreography neatly complements the motivic rhythm here: the Furies frequently jump in the downbeat eighth rests which precede the many repeated eighth-note motives.

From R. 71 through R. 74 the Furies laboriously build a massive structure out of heavy boulders. They strain and bend under the enormous weight. The music supplies some appropriately "heavy" elements: long tenuto notes in strings and horns, two-note descending slurs in the trumpets, trombones and strings after R. 72, and the articulated or repeated eighth-note figure in the horns at R. 71, picked up by the timpani at R. 73.

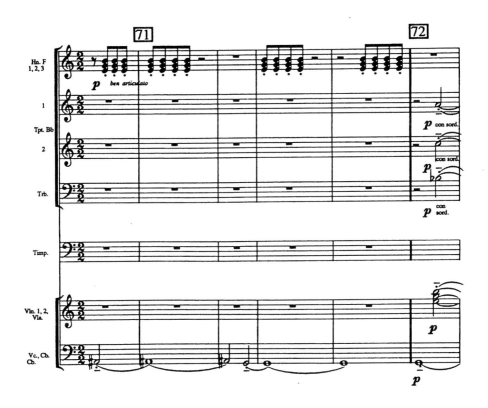

Fig. 12: R. 71 - R. 73 + 1

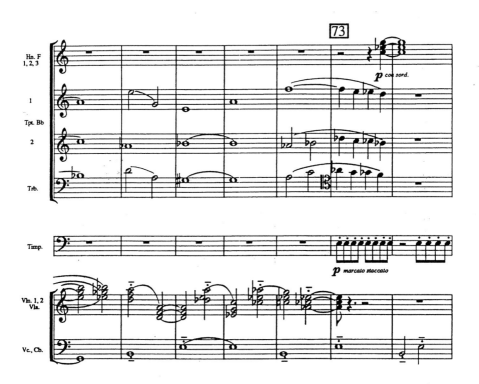

Fig. 12, *continued*

The slow four-note descending motive in trumpets and trombones at R. 73 is particularly effective, and in its contour it is evocative of the harp's original signature motive as well. This entire section is a striking example of archetypal conceit in its musical and choreographic depiction of heaviness. It also exhibits a strong qualitative relationship of tessitura between the heavy, "low" elements of the score and the grounded, "heavy" movements of the boulder lifters.

The second "Air de Danse," beginning at R. 77, provides a strong sense of return to the quality of the opening measures. Although themes and harmonies do not plainly recur, Stravinsky does provide us with the same orchestral texture: solo harp over static, chordal strings. The harp presents an ornamented, diminished variation of its opening motive at R. 77 + 1, roughly inverted and in the Mixolydian mode. At R. 80 a quiet oboe duo heralds the beginning of the famous duet between Orpheus and the Angel. The sinuous lines contain subtle relationships to the original harp motive.

Fig. 13: R. 80 + 1 - 5

The duet continues uninterrupted until R. 88. Again, Stravinsky may be acknowledging Monteverdi's orchestration: the oboes resemble the reedy sound of the *regale*, the distinctive organ which is indicated in the 1615 edition as the preferred continuo instrument during Orfeo's central aria. Another allegorical possibility is that the oboe line, carried on after the Interlude by the English horn, actually represents Orpheus' voice – the bewitching quality of his melodies, and their ability to calm even the tormented souls of Tartarus.

At R. 82 and again at R. 84 Orpheus strums his lyre; but by this point the lyre has become so firmly established as his characteristic instrumental sound in the score, and the mimetic conceit so expected, that only a hint of motion and music are necessary to fulfill the expectation. The entire duet is filled with such instances of understated mimetic conceit.

By R. 88 the theme unravels as Orpheus sinks in despair. As suspected, however, his music has had a calming effect on the tormented inhabitants of Tartarus, who "stretch out their fettered arms toward Orpheus

82

and implore him to continue his song of consolation" during the Interlude (R. 89).[10]

In the conclusion of the "Air de Danse" (after R. 90) the harp and English horn take up the oboe duo's theme in close imitation, gradually becoming more intertwined.

Fig. 14: R. 90 - R. 91

---

[10]Stravinsky 34.

At R. 91 a solo oboe again reiterates the theme for the last time, in diminution. This close, gradually resolving contrapuntal relationship between Orphic and underworld instruments is aptly symbolic: at the end of his Air "Hades, moved by the song of Orpheus, grows calm." The Furies then bind Orpheus' eyes and return Eurydice to him.

Eurydice's dance, starting at the *Poco piu mosso* (R. 94), consists of fitful, halting movements, echoing her anxiety. The music is quite dark – a solo viola plays a mournful, repetitive line while two cellos provide a simple ostinato accompaniment. The emotional parallel in both music and movement is quite obvious.

Fig. 15: R. 94 + 1 - 4

At R. 95, a secondary theme added to music and movement results in a small but effective rhythmic parallel. Violins and trumpets provide soft rhythmic counterpoint with a slurred two-note gesture, often descending by half-step. Each of these gestures is mirrored by a sharp, held movement in Eurydice's dance.

At R. 97 + 3 a bassoon plays a five-note ascending line, starting softly but quickly growing in volume. Stravinsky's use of foreshadowing has already been discussed; yet, surprisingly, the following section which accompanies Orpheus' ascent contains little stepwise ascending movement. Perhaps the composer is setting up an expectation for a musical madrigalism which never comes to pass. In any event, Stravinsky's and Balanchine's contrasting approach to the "ascent" section presents clearly the disparity between a narrative and a non-narrative approach.

At R. 100 Orpheus and Eurydice are reunited.

Orpheus and Eurydice are reunited

Photo: Paul Kolnik

The upper woodwinds play for the first time after a lengthy tacet as the Angel leads the couple and joins their hands together. Flutes and clarinets play a closely related variation of the preceding string ostinato which had accompanied Eurydice's dance. The hand-joining is underscored by a quiet three-chord cadence in the strings.

Fig. 16: R. 100 + 1 - 6

This calm, static cadential statement is one of the most restful moments in the score, and it marks the only point in the story where struggle and tension cease briefly, after Orpheus has successfully won back his lover but before their increasingly difficult ascent from the underworld.

Even in the following "Pas-de-deux," the beginning of which represents the most joyful episode of the story, Stravinsky continues to use fairly dark timbres, employing strings alone. From R. 101 to R. 109 the score maintains a sustained, languid quality, rising only gently as the pair begin their ascent, evolving with restrained intensity not into an ever-higher tessitura, as might be expected, but into a beautiful, chorale-like bed of mid-range string sound. There is underlying tension, however, in the restless, disjunct first violin line from R. 102 to R. 107, punctuated by sustained notes over turgid lower-string movement. This tension can be found in the dynamic of the movement vocabulary as well, where a conflict develops between the joyful play in which the lovers indulge and the struggle between them as Eurydice implores that the mask be removed and Orpheus struggles to keep it on. This struggle is imprinted more clearly in the music after R. 109, when two contrasting and responsorial themes appear: the "playful" theme created by clarinet, timpani and ostinato strings at rehearsals 109, 111 and 114; and the tense "unmasking" theme which accompanies Orpheus' moments of struggle and indecision at rehearsals 110 and 112 in the upper woodwinds, horns, and pizzicato low strings.

Fig. 17: R. 109 to 110 + 4

Fig. 17 *continued*

This section is the most sustained and finely-wrought example of emotional/psychological parallel in the entire work. The feeling of conflict and foreboding, in both choreography and score, is terrifyingly palpable, and Balanchine creates his most poignant images in the lovers' tragic pas-de-deux.

Photo: Paul Kolnik

Orpheus and Eurydice ascend

92

Photo: Paul Kolnik

Eurydice implores Orpheus to remove his mask

At R. 117 the Orphic theme reappears, first in the clarinet, then in the harp, as Eurydice implores Orpheus with renewed vigor. Here his theme works in the opposite direction: whereas previously Orpheus used it to charm the souls of Tartarus, now he is being charmed and implored upon in the same manner.

At R. 118 the previous string "chorale" texture returns. Orpheus, unable to contain himself any longer, tears the mask from his eyes. Eurydice falls dead at his feet.

There is a curious de-dramatization of events in the score immediately preceding Eurydice's death which is difficult to explain in purely narrative terms. This scene represents the climactic, tragic moment of the story, the point where music and movement should logically pay the most respect and heed to the demands of the dramatic action. Yet the constraints of the neoclassical ethos exercise a stronger control here. The poignancy of the chorale-like string theme itself represents a very high level of intensity when viewed in stylistic, not dramatic, context; its texture and tessitura have been carefully controlled. Eurydice's death is accompanied by a full measure of silence just before R. 121. This device alone is a marked contrast to the sustained string lines preceding it. Silence has been used only sparingly in this score, and its judicious placement here produces a profoundly emotional message: the tragedy of sudden loss is beyond the expressive limits of either music or dance.

During the next Interlude, Orphic and underworld instruments mingle as low brass and low strings begin the tragic denouement. The first trumpet plays a staccato, diminished variation of the harp's signature motive at rehearsals 122 and 123.

[Fig. 18: R. 122]

The jarring attacks in the score closely mirror Orpheus' own agitated movements. At R. 124 Orpheus' lyre appears. He bows before it and it is snatched away. He is clearly in a state of rising sorrow and confusion. The ascending dotted-note motive in trumpet and trombone is imitated and enlarged upon by the woodwinds as the emotional conceit builds to a climax.

In the final "Pas d'Action" the leaping arrival of the first Bacchante is announced by loud timpani and pizzicato strings, only the second *fortissimo* dynamic marking in the entire score (the first occurred at the moment of Eurydice's death, just before the measure of silence at R. 121 – 1). At R. 129 + 2, short, sharp brass chords announce the entrance of the main group of Bacchantes.

Fig. 19: R. 129 + 2-3

For the first time, music and movement are equally explosive and dynamic. Choreographer and composer appear intent on releasing the brunt of the pent-up dynamic energy only at this point, choosing not to accentuate the tragic event of Eurydice's death but the far more brutal event of Orpheus' dismemberment. The textural, rhythmic and dynamic relationships in this section are very pronounced and often simultaneous.

In the Apotheosis "Apollo appears, wrests the lyre from Orpheus and raises his song heavenwards."[11] Stravinsky provides a close recapitulation of the opening measures, giving a strong sense of completion to the work. The harp plays a rising ostinato figure at R. 144 as the lyre rises upward. A trumpet solo echoes the harp motive with a meandering but ultimately rising line after R. 148. Curiously, snatches of stepwise descent can still be heard in these final measures in the 2nd horn line, echoing the original harp signature motive.

Fig 20: R. 149 + 1−6

The work ends on a soft D major chord in the strings, with a hint of the seventh in the second violins lending the chord a slightly unfinished, dominantized quality.

What conclusions may be drawn from the patterns of choreomusical relationship we have so painstakingly analyzed in *Orpheus*—conclusions that can help us to better understand the work as a whole? First, it is apparent that certain elements of the Orphic myth were purposely emphasized to reinforce events of dramatic power and to focus on those aspects of the story which most interested the composer and choreographer. Orpheus' musical abilities—his singing and lyre playing—were both obvious choices for musical and choreographic elaboration, resulting in many instances of mimetic conceit. The score's songlike themes, such as the harp's opening motive, are often evocatively lyrical and lie in a middle tessitura, like the male voice.

---

[11]Stravinsky 57.

The lyre playing became an important recurring aural and visual theme, serving as a touchstone or reminder of Orpheus' powers of enchantment. The conflict between the underworld and the real world was also an important thematic *urlinie*. Many instances of archetypal, narrative and emotional/psychological parallel involved this conflict: the imploring "cry and response," the descent, the boulder dance. The orchestrational association of instrumental timbres with characters and locations reinforced many extrinsic choreomusical relationships.

The stronger intrinsic choreomusical relationships – rhythmic, textural, and dynamic – can all be found in sections of high drama, such as Orpheus' dismemberment by the Bacchantes, or group sections, such as the underworld scenes. Choreomusical relationships of all kinds are strongest when the emotional and narrative events of the story need them the most. At certain exciting moments the action may involve many simultaneous categories of affinity.

Yet these relationships, despite the calculated care of their design and placement, never seem arcane or labored. They help to humanize the story, make its resonance transcend the limitations of the non-verbal forms of dance and music. Both choreographer and composer were able to turn a perceived weaknesses of their disciplines – the inability to tell a story through words – into a catalyst for narrative strength. Through the use of choreomusical relationships (and relying, to some degree, on our own pre-existing knowledge of the Orphic myth), Stravinsky and Balanchine were able to sculpt a noble Orpheus in a manner that words never could.

But what kind of Orpheus did these two twentieth-century Russians choose to create? It was not their intent to adhere to the largely optimistic Renaissance revitalization of the Orphic myth as a victory of life over death. Nor was the descent depicted as a voyage of discovery – "Au fond du l'inconnu, pour trouver du nouveau" – as depicted by the nineteenth-century approach to the myth in Nerval or Baudelaire.[12] Orpheus takes nothing with him from his sojourn in Tartarus but his ill-fated lover, and neither score nor

---

[12]Walter A. Strauss, *Descent and Return: The Orphic Theme in Modern Literature* (Cambridge: Harvard University Press, 1971) 220.

choreography acknowledge the type of spiritual growth or rebirth that have characterized Orphic interpretations in literature and music from the sixteenth through late nineteenth centuries. Instead, we are witness to a decidedly fatalistic, even atheistic view: Orpheus as blind fool, unmindful of the powers and limitations of his talent, uncomprehending of the finality of Death, perishing in confusion and powerlessness as his song is denied him. It is a wrenching, dark, and powerful statement, and well-served by the arid tenets of neoclassicism. This Orpheus is stripped of any Romantic notion of redemption, or even the small reward that accompanies the perseverance of dignity in the face of overwhelming loss. In its place is a late twentieth-century morality play which evokes the tone of the original story: actions have consequences, some of them irrevocable, tragic, and all-consuming.

AGON

Choreography by George Balanchine
Score by Igor Stravinsky

Agon, the last part of the Stravinsky-Balanchine trilogy based on classical themes, was almost ten years in the making. Lincoln Kirstein, encouraged by the success of *Orpheus* in 1948, first asked Stravinsky about the possibility of a sequel to complete the cycle in April of that year. The idea was passed back and forth between the two men for the next several years, undergoing a gradual metamorphosis as it shed various early incarnations. Kirstein had suggested as titles *Terpsichore* in 1951, then *Apollo Architectons: builder of shelters and bridges* in 1953. Stravinsky countered with a proposal which was based on the Nausicaa episode from the *Odyssey*. Kirstein and Balanchine then proposed a "competition before the gods," wherein dancers reanimate tired, old gods by performing a series of historical dances – courante, branle, passepied, etc. Suggested Kirstein:

> It is as if time called the tune, and the dances which began quite simply in the sixteenth century took fire in the twentieth and exploded. It would be in the form of a *suite de danses*, or variations, numbers of as great a variety as you pleased.[1]

At about the same time, Kirstein sent Stravinsky a copy of de Lauze's *Apologie de la danse* (1623), a manual with musical examples which Stravinsky studied carefully, sometimes marking (even altering) the accent patterns.

---

[1]Robert Craft, ed., *Stravinsky: Selected Correspondences*, vol. 1 (New York: Knopf, 1982) 287.

Balanchine had his own grandiose ideas for this new ballet, ideas which Kirstein liked to fondly call a "ballet-ivanich": a "ballet to end all ballets" which would include "mad dancing, variations, *pas d'action, pas de deux*, etc. with a final and terrific devastating curtain when everyone would be exhausted."[2]

Stravinsky countered with a suggestion:

> a 'Concerto for the dance' for which George will create a matching choreographic construction. He is a master at this, and has done beautifully with Bizet, Tchaikovsky, Bach, Mozart in music not composed for the dance. So, we can well imagine how successful he will be if given something specially composed for the ballet.[3]

Originally, Stravinsky expected to deliver the finished score for production in November or December of 1954. By August of that year, Stravinsky and Balanchine had worked out, after intense planning sessions together, all the details concerning the ballet's structure. Stravinsky also decided on the name – *Agon* – at about the same time.[4] However, for a number of reasons (mainly the extremely busy schedules of both men), *Agon* did not receive its premiere until December 4, 1957.[5]

Despite its complexity and unwaveringly intellectual, detached aesthetic, *Agon* was an immediate critical and popular success, prompting Kirstein to secure six additional performances. It is frequently remounted both by the New York City Ballet and by other companies, and it remains a universally acknowledged masterwork – arguably the culmination of Stravinsky's and Balanchine's collaborative endeavors.

Agon is virtually brimming with choreomusical affinities of great subtlety and depth; indeed, it is a distillation of Balanchine's methods of

---

[2]Craft 287.

[3]Craft 287.

[4]Vera Stravinsky, interview with Genevieve Oswald, 14 June 1976, New York Public Library, Lincoln Center Dance Collection.

[5]For a more detailed description of *Agon's* creation, see Irene Alm, "Stravinsky, Balanchine, and *Agon*: An Analysis Based on the Collaborative Process," *Journal of Musicology* 7.2 (Spring 1989): 254-256.

assimilating Stravinsky's style and integrating it with his own choreographic intentions to create a powerfully synergistic whole. All of the choreographer's favorite methods of realizing music in movement are here: fast and intricate counterpoint, sustained and close textural and rhythmic parallels, and the choreographic realization of sharply kinetic accent patterns in the music.

An analysis of the original two-piano rehearsal score of *Agon*, with many of the choreographer's instructions annotated in the pianist's (or possibly the choreographer's) hand, reveals a keen awareness of the music's contrapuntal sections and careful attention to polymetric rhythms.[6] Balanchine tried to reflect the music's rhythmic nuances accurately, seldom ignoring the score's important structural points or creating a separate, unrelated series of dance counts, even during difficult polymetric passages. Balanchine never compromised by "squaring off" the counts, nor did he ignore the score's dense rhythmic textures.[7]

Stravinsky's orchestration is extremely spare and economical, typical of many of the works which comprise the last phase of his output. The orchestral forces he chooses, however, are substantial: woodwinds in three's, a full brass choir, harp, mandolin, piano, large percussion battery, and strings. The music is often evocative of seventeenth-century dances, in essence if not in detail: specific forms are slyly suggested, and instrumental combinations often make oblique references to archaic performance practices; the evocations, though, are never literal. More important are the strong intrinsic choreomusical associations developed between dancers and specific instruments. There are consistent and scrupulously observed relationships

---

[6]Igor Stravinsky, Agon, unpublished manuscript for two pianos (New York: Dance Notation Bureau, 1957). Annotations often refer to *Agon's* original dancers by their first names, and so must date from the initial 1957 rehearsal period. According to Irene Alm, "Stravinsky had sent Balanchine a piano score in April 1957, as soon as the music was complete. Balanchine, who was an excellent pianist, learned the score thoroughly, and many times preferred to be his own rehearsal pianist" (Alm 268).

[7]There are, however, several instances in this rehearsal score when simplified "dance counts," regular and repeating number series which ignore polymetric bar lines, were notated. Whether these dance counts were the choreographer's or the dancers' rhythmic crutch is uncertain.

between orchestral and choreographic forces throughout the work, as noted by Irene Alm:

> Stravinsky used full orchestra only in conjunction with the large ensemble numbers at the ballet's opening and close. In the central section, small chamber ensembles of unique instrumental combinations are drawn from the orchestra to complement the solo, duo, and trio dances. Instrumentation also serves to delineate form within pieces, and, to a certain extent, characterizes the dance roles. In general, brass instruments accompany the men and woodwinds are used with the women, although Stravinsky also employs many more subtle nuances.[8]

However, Balanchine does not establish many obvious parallels between characters or identifiable, recurring groups and musical themes in *Agon*. The dancers are treated not as individual characters (as they are in *Orpheus* and *Apollon*) but as nameless components of the choreographic construct, and it is this architecture itself, not a narrative story, which is *Agon's raison d'être*. The story being told is a purely metaphysical one: the beauty of structure and craft, the joy of controlled movement, and the kinetic conflict of opposed bodies. To establish parallels beteen musical themes and individual dancers would have seriously compromised the artists' intent. Rather, we see family relationships, never clear-cut, between musical and choreographic textures and vocabularies – swinging motions, stagewide runs, large leaps and other movements are found to have recognizable musical counterparts – and, as previously noted, a careful matching of musical and choreographic ensemble size.

Balanchine seldom tries to achieve a consistent metrical relationship between movement and music – indeed, considering Stravinsky's predilection for mixed meters, this would have proven quite impractical. Nor, in the opening movement, does Balanchine concern himself with matching choreographic and musical points of accent. Instead, movement and music establish at the outset an easy, loose interdependence, each reflecting the other in less literal ways.

---

[8]Alm 262.

Agon opens with the famous, almost brazen upstage tableau of a male quartet at the beginning of the "Pas-de-Quatre." They stand with their backs to the audience, motionless for a few moments as the curtain rises, then turn downstage in unison before the music begins. Their movements are sharp-edged, kinetic, angular. The music is similarly stark and arid. Sharp-attack instruments predominate: pizzicato strings, piano, harp, and staccato repeated trumpet notes play a pungent and memorable first theme. This quality is perfectly matched to the sharpness of the quartet's movements, particularly the short, quick footwork and brief walking motives, both important elements of Balanchine's choreographic language in this work.

Opening quartet

Photo: Martha Swope

The four-part trumpet-horn counterpoint in mm. 14 to 18 is accompanied by four-part counterpoint in the choreography: the four men perform identical *grand battements* and short side-stepping phrases, each entry delayed by the interval of a quarter note beat.

Figure 1: mm. 14-20

Balanchine doesn't start the choreographic fugue, though, until the entry of the second musical voice – a good example of textural parallel that is not an exact rhythmic relationship. The motoric impulse of the eighth-note-based meters and the recurring sixteenth-note triplets in the lower strings both provide musical support for the walking motives which dominate this first movement. Harp and mandolin often accent the eighth-note pulse during the walking sections, such as in mm. 23 to 25, in precise rhythmic parallel, the dotted-note figures adding a syncopated impulse to the motive.

Fig. 2

Sequential movement patterns return in m. 30, this time triggered by responsorial repeats of the first, repeated-note refrain, now appearing in the clarinet and trumpet lines:

Fig. 3: mm. 30-34

As we shall see, the repeated brass motive in particular, and the brass instruments in general, become associated with the combative, muscular movement themes of the male dancers – the good-natured games of mock combat from which *Agon* derives its title – in an excellent example of thematic timbral relationship.

Measure 39 brings a change of pace: more sustained notes and longer phrases are scored above the energetic, sixteenth-note triplet bassline, and a relaxed, triplet-feel eighth-note motive appears in the brass and woodwinds:

Fig. 4: mm. 39-42

The men's jumping and walking gestures become slower, less bound, yet more weighty, expansive and unified. Despite the appearance of a third contrapuntal section in both score and choreography at m. 46, the qualities of rhythmic relaxation and motivic augmentation dominate the end of this movement, resulting in a beautifully relaxed, symmetrical arm-swinging unison section which elegantly resolves the martial conflict of the contrapuntal movement theme.

The first movement of *Agon* epitomizes the choreomusical ethos of the entire work. Each shift in meter, each melodic contour, each new texture and motive in the score finds its spiritual counterpart in the movement, though the relationships are seldom direct or exact. Like the music, the choreography consists of only three or four simple elements which continually supercede or interrupt each other in a deceptively loose and unstructured pattern: footwork with pizzicato strings, four part movement counterpoint with brass duos, slow arm swings with triplet eighth-note figures, walking motives with sixteenth-note triplets. Because of their deliberate and almost constant misalignment, we sense these intrinsic correspondences on a subliminal or even proprioceptive level, not a literal one.

The second movement is titled "Double Pas-de-Quatre (eight female dancers)." Like many of *Agon's* movements, it overlaps the men's section slightly: the women unobtrusively enter and take their places as the men finish their last movement phrase. We immediately see a close rhythmic correspondence between the women's quick, high *battements* and the thirty-second-note triplet motive in the strings. These kicks, with their attendant extended arm accompaniment, become the visual correspondent to the strings' ostinato figure. The kicks are very rapid and regular, just like the repeated-note string figure. The patterns of the opening sequence are very symmetrical, split neatly on a central axis. The music, too, is very regular through m. 80 – all melodies are phrased to one-bar or half-bar lengths – an obvious structural correspondence.

From "Double Pas-de-Quatre"

Photo: Paul Kolnik

At m. 81 the meter changes from 4/8 to 5/8. Woodwinds set a more lyrical tone with a high melody, marked *tranquillo*, in the flutes. The strings' repeated note figure disappears.

Fig. 5: mm. 81-83

We see a similar change in the dancers' movement style. They perform a series of deep *pliés* and bends, forming a long, unbroken, curved line. The symmetry of the movement gradually becomes less sharply divided, the dancers coming together across the central axis line. The *battements* of the previous section are reinterpreted as well, as long, langorous extensions.

There are several musical parallels to Balanchine's careful symmetry. The orchestration prominently features paired woodwinds, brass, or strings. Only two contrasting moods and themes have been presented as well: the nervous, fluttering theme characterized by the fast triplet figure in the strings, and the more lyrical, slower-paced woodwind theme.

In the complex "Triple Pas-de-Quatre" which follows, scored for eight women and four men, the leg-related movement motives of the first two movements – particularly the quick in-out hip rotation with a slightly bent leg, towards, then away from the body – make a reappearance after the men's introductory leaps. Balanchine opposes three groups, four women/four men/four women, and gives them contrapuntal movement phrases (mainly *battements* with an accompanying side-to-side shifting of the hips). This entire section is a careful and endlessly inventive experiment with group placement. Balanchine's contrapuntal movement motives always contain "high profile" choreography – an abundance of sequential turning, jumping, and dramatic arm movements – making them easy to see, just as a Bach fugue subject contains frequent leaps, disjunct movement, and other inherently dramatic, distinctive characteristics which make it easier to recognize upon its reappearance. Often this contrapuntal movement occurs between groups of paired dancers, two to a movement line.

The hurried, multi-textural orchestration finds its equivalent in the movement patterns–like the music, a mixture of unison, structured counterpoint, and stretto. We see rapidfire examples of rhythmic, structural, textural and dynamic parallel. The quick, incessant thirty-second note figure in the strings contributes to a general feeling of rising tension which dissipates only with the introduction of a relatively relaxed eighth-note theme in violin II at m. 113.

Fig. 6: vln. II, mm. 113-117

At this point the men, having broken off from the larger group, walk through and bisect it as they travel downstage right. The movement ends with a section of tight, integrated, complex symmetry over a woodwind trio-dominated score.

Fig. 7: mm. 118-121

The coda provides welcome relief from the comparative dissonance and hyperactivity of the music and choreography up to this point. This hyperactivity is achieved not through rapidity of movement but by building a complex, additive texture in both music and movement.

The "fussy hands" movement motive, seen elsewhere in this Pas-de-Quatre, returns at the end of the movement at the final cadence/tableau freeze. Consisting of small, seemingly inconsequential movements, it bears some resemblance to the men's "fussy feet" motive at the beginning of their Pas-de-Quatre. Curious, tiny motives such as these often occur at cadential points or other emphatic, structurally important moments in the music, and they provide a drily humorous framing device, hinting, perhaps, that this contest is not to be taken too seriously.

The following "Prelude" presents a series of interesting choreomusical relationships. During the long, carefully orchestrated musical crescendo that comprises the first phrase, the trio (two females, one male) embarks on a series of large, scissors-like kicks and leaps. Then movement and music both change suddenly after m. 131: they become "suspended," as both harmonic rhythm and movement speed slow dramatically to a fraction of the previous tempo.

The following trio, full of elegant tableaux and elaborate bows, seems a parody of courtly dance practices. Stravinsky supplies an appropriately parodic version of a court minuet. The orchestration is strange and bottom-heavy, an eccentric mix of solo contrabasses, harp, timpani, low flutes, and bassoon. We hear frequent quasi-Baroque flourishes and trills, such as the sixteenth-note sextuplet figures in measure 140:

Fig. 8: mm. 136-140

In the "Saraband-Step" of the "First Pas-de-Trois" which follows, the virtuoso movements of the soloists correspond closely to a virtuosic solo violin accompaniment. With its fussy hand movements, large kicks, and athleticism, this movement is reminiscent of earlier scenes. Both choreographer and composer are deliberately ignoring the characteristics of the traditional Sarabande – its slow courtliness and emphasis on the second beat of every measure.

The "Gailliarde" for two female dancers is provided with a curious score, arranged to sound like some strange, ancient consort of indeterminate orchestration. Strings, harp, mandolin, and flutes playing soft harmonics create a charmingly out-of-tune quality, sounding not unlike an ancient portative organ. Renaissance influences can be heard in the melodic patterns as well.

Fig. 9: mm. 164-165

By this time, much of the movement material is familiar: the "in-out" leg swings, the fussy hands and arms at the final cadence. The dance movement is highly attuned to the music's accents and cadences, especially the numerous syncopations which delay the downbeat by an eighth note.

The lively "Coda," for one male and two females, is, like the Gailliarde, very symmetrical. Jumps and sharp in-out leg movements correspond to a sharply pointillistic score. Each of the trio's series of jumps is initiated by an upward-sliding *glissando* in the solo cello line. All major movements are aligned with a pointed, regular ostinato (every dotted quarter note in 6/8 meter). Balanchine sets up a strong, heterotextural rhythm; this is a common characteristic of his quick-tempo group sections (think, for example, of the Underworld scenes in *Orpheus*), wherein different, sharply rhythmic movement events occur simultaneously, each assigned to only one or two dancers, with points of close imitation among them, creating a dense and complex texture. The movement here consists of arms and legs thrown up energetically, accompanied by sharp changes of balance and the back-forth shifting of both pelvis and hips. Balanchine allows the points of imitation to become closer and closer, until finally the section ends with a unison phrase. This texture is introduced only when the music itself has become strongly heterophonic, even contrapuntal. The close correspondence of music and movement events in this section adds greatly to its satisfying athleticism – especially the humorous touches, such as the combination of a rapidly descending melodic line (mm. 243-244) with quickly lowered torsos.

The "Interlude" reiterates the violent orchestrational crescendo last heard in the "Prelude." This time, though, the sexes of the trio are reversed, with two males and one female. After a precise, unison upstage entrance, the trio performs a series of slow turns and freezes, with the woman balanced between the two men, in much the same manner as the "Prelude".

"Interlude"   Photo: Martha Swope

118

This time, the allusion to pre-Classic dance practices seems even more pronounced, as the woman is delicately maneuvered into several visually beautiful *relevé* balances. The movement here is, in fact, a mirror image of that in the "Prelude": the dancers start on the opposite side of the stage, and their sex ratio is reversed.

In the "Second Pas-de-Trois" we see three dances, titled "Bransle Simple," "Bransle Gay" and "Bransle Double". Like the Renaissance Bransle, these dances do have their moments of energy, though the similarity is broadly drawn at best.

In the "Bransle Simple" we see a clear example of textural parallel. The section begins with two trumpets in very close imitation.

Fig. 10: mm. 278-281

Two male dancers mirror the counterpoint. There is, however, one subtle yet important difference between musical and choreographic counterpoint. In the movement, the counterpoint is displaced by a quarter note; in the music, by a half note. A phrase of spiky, angular unison movement ensues, accompanied by a spare score which features paired clarinets, continuing the textural parallel between musical and choreographic duet. Quick points of rhythmic parallel can be spotted between the duo's leaps and the *pizzicato* chords in the strings. Balanchine never allows himself to become completely dependent, though, on the music as an initiator of fast, kinetic movement. The accentual peaks and valleys of score and choreography are similar, but as we might expect they seldom match.

The "Bransle Gay" is a solo for female dancer. We see the reappearance of the familiar scissors-like leg motive, as the spare score provides a simple accompaniment of paired flutes, paired bassons, harp and castanet; later it broadens slightly to include paired clarinets and strings. The clacking castanet provides a characteristic, slow flamenco rhythm, not what one would expect of a Bransle.

Fig. 11: mm. 310-311

A single man upstage right mirrors the castanet rhythm with clapping (though silent) hands, an excellent example of mimetic conceit. His presence, adhering to the flamenco tradition, further enhances the association. The woman's dance consists of a series of fluid movements which are structured in extraordinarily short phrases, corresponding exactly to the phrasing of the slow 3/8 accompaniment – an example of unusual structural parallel because of the extreme brevity of the movement phrases. The music is complex and polymetric, yet the castanet's simple ostinato keeps it deceptively regular and dancelike. Many of the dancer's other movements recall the flamenco movement style as well: fluid upper body motion, especially in the arms, and frequent changes of facing. The solo gradually becomes more rapid and technically demanding. Movements, often on *pointe*, occur every sixteenth note toward the end of the section. Music and movement are both spare, elegant, and brimming with compressed, tightly directed energy.

The final "Bransle Double," for two males and one female, begins with strident and comparatively full music as the woman is thrown vertically from man to man. *Agon's* predominant thematic parallelism imbues this moment: scissory leg movements and robust jumps match the masculine, brass-accented score. A piano-dominated second theme, slightly less active than the first, appears in the music at m. 352.

120

Fig. 12: mm. 352-355

It is accompanied by a favorite Balanchinian slow movement technique, dating back, at least, to *Apollon Musagète*: the tableau-freeze. The two men stand upstage center, arms extended, while the woman dances immediately downstage of them.

"Bramsle Double"   Photo: Paul Kolnik

A similar phrase emerges at the end of this section. The movement becomes slow and circular as the dancers execute an elaborate "daisy chain" turn, each passing inside the ring of arms, from mm. 373 to 386 in the score. The music's harmonic rhythm again slows and the score becomes, like the dance, circular and non-directional. Stravinsky ends this section with a short, percussive cadence, even though there is no corresponding movement in the choreography. The composer seems intent on making all structural points clear and unequivocal, letting us know that this is a series of variations with sharply defined parameters, both stylistically and temporally.

After an "Interlude" (identical to the two previous ones and with similar choreographic material) comes the final "Pas-de-deux". This section is the triumphant culmination of *Agon's* spare, beautiful aesthetic – in both score and choreography, a moment of distillation and repose, where the sharp pointillism of the music is reflected in movement vocabulary of extreme economy, such as the woman's precise and jaggedly elegant pointework. There is an emphasis on balance and the suspension of weight; movements are slow, deliberate.

"Pas-de-deux"   Photo: Paul Kolnik

One could argue that this is only the second point in the ballet where a convincing extrinsic thematic choreomusical relationship exists. The tension and conflict of the male-female relationship, so profoundly different from the boisterous all-male conflicts of the first movement, is laid bare and explored, both in the extremely careful, convoluted and sinewy movement, filled with delicate yet tense moments of suspension and balance, and in the dry, haunting dissonance and judiciously placed silences of the music. This section is scored for strings alone, and solo violin and viola are frequently pitted against each other in effective textural parallel to the dancers' duet.

It is perhaps too easy to apply sex role- and emotion-based rationales to this section simply because it is the only extended male-female duet in *Agon*. But the implications are nevertheless plain: the man supports and suspends the woman, always gently controlling her movement, sometimes even deliberately placing her feet with his hands. The man is frequently below the woman, either kneeling or lying on the ground, as if in supplication. Tremolo violins at mm. 447-448 find their choreographic reflection in the man's quick, shuffling foot movements.

From m. 452 until the end of the section, the pace of both the choreographic and musical events increases suddenly. The pent-up tension of the duo is released in a series of dramatic leg-split slides, the man supporting the woman as she falls.

Horns return in the following male solo beginning in m. 463, reminding us of the association of brass instruments with the themes of masculine athleticism and competition.

Fig. 13: mm. 463-467

The man's movements are strident, forceful; the woman watches. The woman's short solo, composed of now-familiar leg-oriented material, is accompanied by a change of orchestration: brass instruments disappear, and a flute trio plays a gentle eighth-note melody, accompanied by a simple string ostinato pattern.

Fig. 14: mm. 473-476

As expected, the horns return when the male dancer resumes his solo at m. 484.

With the appearance of the mandolin at m. 504, the male-female duet becomes more tender and the woman takes a more active role in the choreographic shape-making. Still, the element of masculine control is evident: the man pushes the woman's foot slowly into an *arabesque* position with his hand. Nevertheless, as the "pas-de-deux" ends, music and movement have both softened subtly but noticeably.

In the next section, titled "Four Duos," strident, often brass-dominated music and sharply pointillistic effects in both score and choreography result in pronounced textural, dynamic and rhythmic parallels. Music and movement are both monotextural; the movement features tightly controlled unison.

In the following "Four Trios," the upper/lower string fugue is paralleled closely by the movement, the second group of dancers imitating the first. However, the choreographic points of imitation are faster than their musical counterparts. The four trios engage in counterpoint of rapidly increasing complexity as the musical texture erupts into stretto at m. 545.

The "Coda" evolves cleverly out of the large group's symmetrical tableau. By the time the familiar repeated brass chords (an elaboration of *Agon's* opening motive) are heard, the four men have broken off from the group and move downstage, playing out their own symmetrical phrase. The "Coda," a fully harmonized version of the original brass theme, accompanies similarly recapitulative movement, complex and symmetrical, involving all twelve dancers. All the important choreographic elements of the ballet seem to be replayed simultaneously: close counterpoint, the fussy hand and foot movements, male stridency.

Fig. 15: mm. 561-568

At m. 574 we see a highly developed example of a distinctly Balanchinian choreomusical trait: as the brass presents a contrapuntal line, stage-symmetrical contrapuntal entries are seen in the movement. Two to four dancers on each side of the center line perform identical movement phrases in quick succession, usually highly visible and dramatic.

"Coda"

Photo: Paul Kolnik

This highly symmetrical choreography ends with an elegant recapitulation of the male quartet's original movement motive, ending upstage center as they had begun, to the same music.

What is it that moves us so profoundly about *Agon*, so uncompromisingly abstract in aesthetic and conception, yet so robust, humorous and joyous in execution? It is easy to sense, even without an analysis such as this, that Stravinsky and Balanchine have achieved in *Agon* an elegant parallelism in their treatment of both ethos and pathos. In all aspects, the work is a masterpiece of matched artistic intent and purity of vision. Both men adhere to the same constructive dictates: strongly rhythmic gestures, the artful use of stasis/silence and counterpoint, textural variety, and economy of means. Both men restrain their respective vocabularies, limiting themselves to only the most essential expressive tools for the task.

Yet the result is anything but rigid or constrictive. *Agon* is a fount of inventiveness, its subtleties unfolding gradually with each successive viewing. It gracefully epitomizes the qualities we have come to associate with Stravinsky/Balanchine collaborations in the precision and cool, almost offhanded masterfulness of its music-movement affinities. It stands alone as the last great collaboration between the two men (their only notable later effort, *The Flood* [created in 1962 for NBC television] was an admitted failure, a victim of insufficient collaborative time, the absence of an inspired catalyst such as Lincoln Kirstein, and the brutal dictates of commercial television).[9] *Agon* will undoubtedly continue to enjoy a reputation as one of the greatest ballets, and one of the finest examples of collaboration between choreographer and composer, that this century has yet produced.

---

[9]For additional information about *The Flood* and its creative genesis, see Igor Stravinsky, George Balanchine and Robert Craft, "Notes for *The Flood*," Eugene Burdick et al., eds., *The Eighth Art: 23 Views of Television Today* (New York: Holt, Rinehart & Winston, 1962) 261-269; also "Noah and the Flood," *Dance and Dancers* (July 1962): 10-14.

BILLY THE KID

Choreography by Eugene Loring

Score by Aaron Copland

Since his demise in 1881 at the age of 21, Billy the Kid has ascended to the pantheon of American cultural icons – at first glance an unlikely candidate for that honor. True, his criminal exploits were reported regularly by the newspapers of the western territories, but only as a footnote to the ongoing Lincoln County cattle wars, in which he was a minor player. Billy's mythologizing occured in the second-hand descriptions of the eastern press, striving to keep its curious readers abreast of all the news, true, exaggerated, or fictitious, from the wild and woolly western frontier. Stories abounded: he had killed his first man at twelve; he had killed twenty-one men, one for every year of his young life; he killed for sport; he had a sweetheart in every hacienda; he was an excellent marksman, able to shoot a target over his shoulder by looking at a small hand-held mirror; he was extremely courteous to women and children.[1]

This mythologizing process has proven to be an indispensible step in the creation of a cultural icon – a personality who becomes embedded in the collective consciousness of a society. Billy the Kid scholar Stephen Tatum notes:

---

[1]For a more detailed description of Billy's alleged exploits (as opposed to the known facts of his life), see Stephen Tatum, "An Introduction to Billy the Kid's Legend and Bibliography" in *Inventing Billy the Kid* (Albuquerque: University of New Mexico Press, 1982) 3-14.

As with Buffalo Bill, Custer, and Jesse James, Billy the Kid's persistent presence in our imagination demonstrates an appeal that crosses and recrosses any supposedly firm boundaries between the folk, the popular, and the artistic imaginations, or any conventional boundaries between history and legend. Because every generation and every culture creates figures who embody the preoccupations of the moment, the Kid may not be as immediately important as any cultural hero of the moment, any Lindbergh or Luke Skywalker, but the Kid has endured like the classical figure Proteus, the "shape-shifter" who eludes the death-grips of his antagonists by changing forms as the situation demands.[2]

So much has been written about Eugene Loring and Aaron Copland's *Billy the Kid*, and so many contradictory statements made about its conception,[3] that, like Billy himself, the descriptions of the birth of this seminal American ballet assume almost mythical qualities.

Apparently, Loring's initial attitude toward Copland's abilities as a composer for ballet was not entirely positive, although that quickly changed:

When I first joined Ballet Caravan, I began to get to know, through Kirstein, a lot of painters and photographers and musicians. That's how I met Aaron Copland. At that point he had already done some ballets for Ruth Page [actually only one, *Hear Ye! Hear Ye!*, 1934] – they weren't very good. As it turned out, *Billy* was his first successful one...for me, working with Copland was very clear cut, mutually productive.[4]

A lengthy and thorough working-out process involved close collaboration between Loring and Copland. Says Loring, "I had never been west of the Mississippi, but I did an outline, and after Copland got involved, we filled in the action."[5] After deciding on principal incidents and a climax, Loring estimated the approximate duration of each event. Copland then

---

[2]Tatum 5-6.

[3]Richard Philip (in "*Billy the Kid* Turns Fifty," *Dance Magazine* November 1988: 42) credits Lincoln Kirstein with the libretto; yet Eugene Loring insists that he, not Kirstein, wrote the story for *Billy* (see Aaron Copland and Vivian Perlis, *Copland 1900-1942* [New York: St. Martin's/Marek, 1984] 280, and Eugene Loring, interview with Marilyn Hunt [NYPL Dance Collection Oral History Archive, 1976] 35.)

[4]Philip 50.

[5]Aaron Copland and Vivian Perlis, *Copland 1900-1942* (New York: St. Martin's/Marek, 1984) 280.

composed "musical ideas," or thematic sketches, for each incident. On several occasions, Copland prevailed Loring to try concepts about which the choreographer initially felt some apprehension. Loring had reservations about the introductory March, for example – unlike most marches, it is in a triple meter – but Copland convinced him that the spirit of the march was what mattered, and the choreographer finally deemed it appropriate.

Copland also possessed an excellent sense of thematic potential. He would often tell Loring that a musical idea which the choreographer liked could unfortunately not be developed for the length of time the scene demanded. He was also very adept at the craft of "custom fitting" the score: during the rehearsal process he made frequent cuts and extensions to the music, with little apparent loss of seamlessness or organicism in the finished product.[6]

Billy the Kid was first staged by Lincoln Kirstein's Ballet Caravan at the Chicago Opera House on October 16, 1938, with the choreographer himself in the title role. Aaron Copland's elegantly simple description of the libretto is often quoted:

> The action begins and closes on the open prairie. The central portion of the ballet concerns itself with significant moments in the life of Billy the Kid. The first scene is a street in a frontier town. Familiar figures amble by. Cowboys saunter into town, some on horseback, others with their lassoes. Some Mexican women do a *Jarabe* which is interrupted by a fight between two drunks. Attracted by the gathering crowd, Billy is seen for the first time as a boy of twelve with his mother. The brawl turns ugly, guns are drawn, and in some unaccountable way, Billy's mother is killed. Without an instant's hesitation, in cold fury, Billy draws a knife from a cowhand's sheath and stabs his mother's slayers. His short but famous career had begun. In swift succession we see episodes in Billy's later life.
>
> At night, under the stars, in a quiet card game with his outlaw friends. Hunted by a posse led by his former friend Pat Garrett. Billy is pursued. A running gun battle ensues. Billy is captured.
>
> A drunken celebration takes place. Billy in prison is, of course, followed by one of Billy's legendary escapes. Tired and worn

---

[6]For a more complete description of Loring and Copland's collaborative process, see Eugene Loring, interview with Marilyn Hunt (New York City Public Library Dance Collection) 43-44.

out in the desert, Billy rests with his girl. Starting from a deep sleep, he senses movement in the shadows. The posse has finally caught up with him. It is the end.[7]

Eugene Loring allowed himself the liberty of a Protean Billy, reshaping the man and the myth in ways which would suit his own choreographic and intellectual needs, and consequently artistic licence has been invoked throughout Loring and Copland's retelling of the legend. For one thing, Billy's mother was not really killed in a gun battle, nor did Billy kill "in cold fury" as a result.[8] Billy was ambushed and killed by Garrett not in the desert, but at the ranch home of the father of one of his lady friends.[9]

Copland, as well, omits several important details in his description. Loring makes it clear that the appearance of Billy's sweetheart in the desert near the end is a dream sequence, nothing more.[10] Loring takes pains to create an ethereal figure: her pointework makes her unique among the ballet's characters. She is the most traditionally balletic character of the work, and the least indigenously Western in appearance. Also omitted by Copland is an important narrative detail: Garrett appears early in the story, offering vain assistance to the young Billy after the death of his mother. Thus the final minutes of the ballet, dealing with Garrett's capture, pursuit and killing of Billy, achieve an important dramatic irony.

Copland's score is orchestrated for a medium-sized orchestra: woodwinds in pairs, four horns, three trumpets, three trombones, tuba, timpani, percussion, harp, piano, and strings. The simple and stark opening motive is repeated several times, each time with a different orchestration.

---

[7]Copland, "Notes on a Cowboy Ballet," *Billy the Kid* Ballet Suite (New York: Boosey & Hawkes, 1941) ii; reprinted in Neil Butterworth, *The Music of Aaron Copland* (London: Toccata Press, 1985) 77.

[8]Tatum 19.

[9]Tatum 33-34.

[10]Loring interview 59, 60.

Fig. 1: mm. 1-6

Loring presents us with a slowly moving tableau of archetypal Western pioneers, each engaged in an activity of some kind: roping, riding, etc. There are five separate activities in all, each repeated in canonic fashion, as the group moves slowly but inexorably "westward" – from the audience's right to their left. This march is reiterated again at the end of the ballet, and it creates a magnificent framing device, making Billy's story seem an inevitable part of a much larger and vastly more important mythology, the taming of the West.

Opening March tableau

Photo: Donald Bradburn

The clarity and simplicity of each movement phrase allow us to imagine all the trappings of a Western fable purely through the power of suggestion. Said Loring:

> I decided that by recalling the wonderful imagery everyone uses in their childhood, it would be easy to recognize the suggestions of guns, horses, and card playing.[11]

It is through the careful, stylized conveyance of familiar activities in this prologue march that we are familiarized with the elegant, spare, yet highly communicative language of the work. Loring has carefully avoided contrived or overtly mimetic action; we are introduced to each activity through a kind of movement shorthand. Thus a dancer hopping in deep *plié*, legs spread into a wide fifth position, skipping slowly forward in a R-R-L-R, L-L-R-L pattern, becomes a man on horseback (see photo, p. 140).

---

[11]Eugene Loring, narration for Omnibus telecast of *Billy the Kid*, November 1953, ts., (University of California, Irvine, Special Collections) n.p.

Billy and a rider   Photo: Donald Bradburn

Through the judicious construction of such movement motives, Loring eliminates the need for props of any kind. More importantly, he uses the very familiarity of the movement as a platform upon which to build a story of subtlety and complexity. Since the movement sources could be termed American vernacular, he is free to redefine them, disguise them, or use them in search of a deeper level of meaning without fear of losing his audience.

Copland has devised a similar aesthetic approach in the musical vocabulary of the score. Familiar songs of the Old West, such as "Goodbye Old Paint," "Great Grand-Dad," "The Old Chisolm Trail," and "Git Along Little Dogies" are presented in recognizable but subtly altered form. Said Copland:

> It is a delicate operation to put fresh and unconventional harmonies to well-known melodies without spoiling their naturalness; moreover, for an orchestral score, one must expand, contract, rearrange and superimpose the bare tunes themselves, giving them something of one's own touch.[12]

Thus each tune is subjected to the rigorous structural and textural techniques of serious composition; yet the result is natural, unforced, and Copland's treatments of the tunes never overwhelm them. Their simple, uncluttered melodies are never lost to the listener.

In those parts of the score which are free-composed, Copland devised an elegantly sophisticated language which is perfectly compatible with the folk tunes without sacrificing harmonic or textural complexity. When setting crucial moods, such as at the beginning of the introductory March, the composer makes use of gently stated perfect fifths in the woodwinds and a modal, short phrased melody with no easily definable tonal center – the perfect musical counterpart to the existential emptiness and moral uncertainty of the nineteenth-century prairie which Loring was trying to express. Lincoln Kirstein feels "his [Copland's] lonely, spare, sweet harmonies suggest the weather, the earth and space of western territory very

---

[12] Copland and Perlis 279.

actively."[13] Thus movement, scenery and score work in tandem to create archetypal conceits at important, mood-setting moments.

Copland was not afraid of using silence to make an important point. "I have never liked music to get in the way of the thing it is supposedly aiding," he has said; "...the eye is the thing, and music must play a more modest role."[14] The score is filled with extended sections of silence. Most important, perhaps, are the silences which accompany each of Billy's acts of murder. Composer and choreographer agreed that at these moments, silence was more eloquent than any sound. In fact, the only two places in *Billy* where music accompanies a killing are during the murder of Billy's mother, and during the execution of Billy himself – the latter, though, is preceded by several minutes of silence and features a mimetic conceit in the orchestra several seconds *after* Pat Garrett's deadly volley hits its mark.[15]

The introductory March is followed after a brief blackout by the first scene of the narrative proper, set in a small desert town. Copland provides a saucy, playfully dissonant theme for muted piccolo and tin whistle.

Fig. 2: R. 6 1-12

We are introduced to several disparate groups of people in the first few minutes of this scene, all with identifying movement motives, many with their own characteristic musical themes or thematic variations:

---

[13]Lincoln Kirstein, "About *Billy the Kid,*" *The Dance Observer* (October 1938): 116.

[14]Copland and Perlis 279.

[15]Loring interview 54.

– the Mexican: a dignified figure, he maintains a slow, regal walk – perhaps he is on a slowly moving horse;

– the riders and the buckaroo: their riding motives each receive distinctive, rhythmically appropriate musical treatment;

– the dance hall girls: their flamboyant, slightly bawdy steps are danced to a variation of the scene's opening theme in an implied 5/2 (not indicated, however, in the time signature); the trombone appears for the first time here as a melody instrument. They mark the fourth beat of each phrase with an emphatic shake of their tail feathers, the music providing a corresponding accent:

Fig. 3: R. 10 + 4 – 9

– the dancing rodeo cowboys: their masculine choreography includes much unison movement; unison strings provide them with a texturally appropriate background;

– the dancing Mexican girls: their *Jarabe*[16] is accompanied by a spirited, appropriately Mexican sounding tune in a tricky 5 + 4 meter. Music and movement both capture the essence of *folklorico* dancing without striving for literal authenticity;

---

[16]The *Jarabe* is a popular Mexican dance dating from the late Colonial period. It is derived from the traditional *jarabe*, one of the oldest folkdances of Mexico, usually triple in meter with occasional bars of 6/8. Since the nineteenth century it has been adopted by salon and popular musicians, and in this later form it is characterized by a fast tempo, alternating 6/8 and 3/4 meters, frequent melodic syncopation, harmonization in thirds and sixths, and simple tonic-dominant harmonic patterns. It is binary in form, with 8, 16, or 24 bars for each *son* (tune).

The Jarabe

Photo: Donald Bradburn

Fig. 4: R. 20 1-12, tpts only

As the scene evolves, two characteristics of the score and choreography become apparent. One is the skill with which Copland and Loring have created and sustained instances of archetypal conceit, particularly concerning the depiction of horse riding. A buckaroo gallops off quickly, utilizing the fast quarter note beat unit of the music as the rhythmic impetus of his gallop. Immediately two riders canter in upstage right, their slower gait timed to the dotted half note, the trumpets providing a hemiola in threes to signify the unique feel of the horses' canter.

Fig. 5: R. 9 + 8-13, tpt. 2 and 3 only

Later, the buckaroo enters on a wildly bucking bronco. The music here is scored for loud, full orchestra. The unpredictable rhythmic accents and polyrhythms of the score work in close rhythmic parallel with the mimetic choreography to imitate the wild, jerking dance of an untamed horse.

The second musical element is less immediately noticeable because it is so skillfully employed: the organic ease with which Copland's themes coalesce, dissipate, and run together according to the narrative dictates of the action. Copland switches expertly and seamlessly between disparate styles, textures and time signatures as each character or group appears in turn. Some examples: the dance hall girls' theme breaks up into small rhythmic fragments and motivic repetition as they exit in a fragmented manner upstage right. The rodeo cowboys mingle with the dance hall girls as they exit; immediately the music recapitulates a small phrase of the original "playful" motive, scored for muted trumpet and two oboes, as they flirt. The accompaniment for the *Jarabe* smoothly shifts from a complex polyrhythm to

4/4 as "Goodbye Old Paint" returns. The score is organic, continuous, and succeeds in linking this community of diverse personalities tightly together.

Twelve-year-old Billy is introduced twice during this scene: first as he enters, tentatively and with a child's curiosity, clutching his mother's dress as the score reiterates the sprightly jig which opened the scene; and later on, entering from upstage left, carrying his mother playfully as the music introduces a rendition of "Goodbye Old Paint." The song underscores the rest of the scene, transforming slowly as events build to their terrible climax.

Copland has set "Goodbye Old Paint" with a soft yet insistent accent on the second beat of each bar of 3/4, imparting it with a lilting, offbeat quality. The orchestration is gentle and understated as Billy and his mother dance. Solo oboe and strings predominate. Gradually the orchestrational thickness increases and contrapuntal lines begin to appear as the focus of the scene widens and the townsfolk are again seen, each group occupied with its own movement motives – a clearly structured textural parallel. As the activity increases, so too does a feeling of apprehension, apparent most obviously in the rising dynamic level of the score. A fight breaks out between two men. The syncopated, regular accent on the second beat of each measure of "Old Paint" becomes progressively more heavy, gradually overwhelming the melodic rhythm. The music feels strangely off-balance, just as the two fighting men are often thrown off-balance. As the fight becomes more frenzied, the choreographic energy of the fight spills over into the townspeople – many arms begin to flail, movement activity increases. A rolling suspended cymbal parallels the rising tension. Suddenly, Billy's mother falls dead, victim of a stray bullet from one of the fighting men.

148

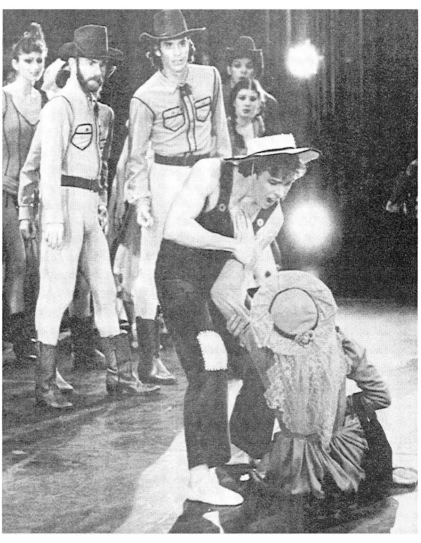

Death of Billy's Mother   Photo: Donald Bradburn

Copland's handling of this moment is not mimetic – he offers no aural counterpart to the clearly mimed gunshots. Instead, the score provides a more subtle psychological/emotional parallel: starting a moment after the Mother is hit, a dissonant chord is struck three times, each time decreasing in volume, as life drains from her. It is followed by an extended silence, during which Billy, in a rage, grabs a knife and stabs the killer once in the back. The music resumes only after the cowboy's death.[17] These powerful, horrific images need no accompaniment; they speak for themselves.

"Old Paint" takes on a dirgelike quality as the scene ends. It appears for the first time without rhythmic alteration as the Mother is carried offstage. The melody becomes increasingly augmented, then fragmented, as the townspeople slowly, haltingly resume their activities after witnessing the murders. The accent has now shifted from the second to the third beat of each measure.

This entire sequence, from the second entrance of Billy and his mother to the end of the scene, is a sustained and carefully controlled masterpiece of choreomusical association. Copland and Loring build a slowly tightening latticework of tension through textural, dynamic, rhythmic, and particularly psychological/emotional parallel. The absence of any music at the very climax of the scene allows the audience to feel the level of horror and poignance for itself, without the crutch of an intrusive score.

In the next scene we see the adult Billy – confident, contemptuous, and full of deadly energy. It is here that we are first introduced to Billy's "rage" motive, described chillingly by Olga Maynard as his "spiral of ecstasy."[18] Gun drawn, he spins around rapidly, facing downstage.

---

[17]Apparently this silence was added late in the collaborative process, as Copland's two piano rehearsal score in his own hand (ms., Dance Notation Bureau reproduction, 1986, p. 21, mm. 293-300) indicates a light underscore was to be played during the stabbing.

[18]Olga Maynard, *The American Ballet* (Philadelphia: Macreae Smith Company, 1959) 166.

150

Billy's "rage" motive   Photo: Donald Bradburn

The music is dissonant, dominated by an insistent, simple trumpet melody. A posse rides by. Billy shoots one of them. The score builds up to this moment in quick crescendo, but the moment of the shot itself is silent. There is the barest minimum of underscore as Billy kicks the body, turning it over. Then Billy does a curious thing: he marks out very stylized, almost ritualistic movement patterns, jumping over the body as he does so. It is a confusing and controversial moment. Loring explains it as a moment of revulsion – Billy is filled with sudden remorse for his wrongdoing, and pays macabre penance over the body.[19] As with the killing, this ritual is played out in silence.

A variation of the March theme opens the next scene.

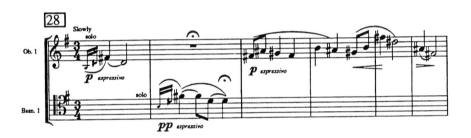

Fig. 6: R. 28 + 1 – 6

The music is subdued, in the modal minor. Solo oboe and bassoon, then strings, outline the melody. Billy is playing cards on the open prairie with his friend, Pat Garrett. The scene is peaceful, intimate – interestingly, the only other time we saw Billy in a happy mood (with his mother in the second scene), oboe and strings were the predominant orchestrational texture.

Billy engages in a rhythmic duet with his card-playing partner. Its internal rhythms, marked by hand slapping and foot stomping, have nothing to do rhythmically or dynamically with the quiet, unmetered trumpet solo. Trumpet, as well, has been used before with Billy's character in conjunction with his violent predilections, and it serves here as a foreshadowing device.

---

[19]Loring interview 52.

Copland seems to be building subtle thematic relationships, not only between specific characters and instruments, but between instruments and the precise moods of a particular character.

Immediately after Garrett's departure, a running gun battle erupts. Copland draws us into the new mood through the use of a single unison note in the strings which rapidly grows in volume. The next sequence is filled with instances of mimetic conceit, as the shots of the posse are echoed in the scattergun, unpredictable "shots" of orchestral punctuation, consisting of short, massed chords for low strings, brass and percussion and loud rat-a-tat rim shot interjections by the snare drum. The music is suffused with the feeling of violence, danger and loud noise.

Fig. 7: R. 33 + 1–6

154

The points of mimetic imitation, however, are never exact; rather, it is the cumulative effect which convinces us of the parallelism of action and sound. There is a strong psychological/emotional correspondence operating here as well – music and movement impel each other to ever higher levels of tension, culminating in the capture of Billy.

Once again, though, an important moment transpires in silence: as he is led away, Billy kills another man before his capturer can stop him. The killing takes place without music, and the silence remains as he and Garrett ride off to jail.

A celebratory *danse macabre* emerges from the silence, its absurdness made more acute by its proximity to this senseless murder. Piccolo and oboe outline the melody.

Fig. 8: R. 40 + 1 – 10

Celebratory *danse macabre*

Photo: Donald Bradburn

The annoying banality of the music soon gives way to wild abandon. Dissonances and strange instrumental doublings are heard as the members of the posse, now joined by some of the townsfolk, dance drunkenly and jubilantly in celebration of Billy's capture. Even dead bodies briefly become part of the dancing party, propped up by others. Movement and music both convey a strange, unsettling subtext to this merriment. The phrasing of the music is not square; melodies are disjunct and unpredictable, orchestration calculatedly eccentric; the piccolo screeches near the top of its range; the choreography is awkward, off-balance, and heavy. The entire dance is a deftly handled instance of emotional/psychological parallel.

In the next scene, we see Billy in jail, playing cards with his jailer.

Billy playing cards with his jailer   Photo: Donald Bradburn

The slow, innocuous clarinet melody, with a noodling countermelody for bassoon, texturally parallels the two characters onstage. The relaxed music, however, is at odds with Billy's emotional state – he clicks his heels loudly as he deals the cards, belying an inner tension. The scene ends with the killing of the jailer – identical to the others, played out in silence.

The last scene of the narrative part of *Billy* takes place in the desert at night. Copland provides a mysterious new theme for strings and harp, which raises the viewer's level of apprehension.

A posse approaches, accompanied by a trumpet solo (trumpet solos in the past have been associated with Billy's anger and aggressiveness). Billy eludes them by taking refuge behind two Mexican girls as the posse rides by. He meets an Indian guide in the desert; the mysterious music prevails. Billy beds down for the night. Billy's sweetheart appears in the darkness. Is she real? Billy ignores or does not see her.

Billy's sweetheart appears   Photo: Donald Bradburn

She dances a delicate solo to a slow waltz. Finally he awakens and they dance together as the waltz grows in intensity.

The final part of the scene, the climax of the story, is performed entirely in silence – a brave decision on Copland's part. Garrett stealthily searches for Billy. He stumbles; Billy starts. They circle the stage, backs to each other. Billy calls out to the night: "*Quien es?*" Relieved at hearing nothing, he lights a match for a cigarette. Garrett fires at the light; Billy dies.

Billy dies   Photo: Donald Bradburn

At this very moment, the score returns–short, percussive bursts of brass and percussion, similar to the Mother's death motive. Choreographically and musically, the deaths of Billy and his mother are very similar.

A brief eulogizing ceremony takes place as maidens enter and pass upstage left to right in a strictly orthographic pattern. Strings alone play a quiet hymnlike accompaniment in slow 4/4 time.

Billy ends with a reprise of the opening March. The choreography has been varied slightly–it is somewhat more tentative in its direction than the initial March, and the backward-facing turn of each dancer passes quickly through the group, like wind whipping through a field of grain, as the curtain falls.[20]

Billy the Kid has been called the first significant wholly "American" ballet–the first ballet about an American subject, created by American artists, and, most important, reflective of a new and identifiably American aesthetic. Richard Philip notes:

> *Billy* was the first fully realized ballet treatment of a new American idiom that consciously turned its back on the Franco-Russian heritage (particularly the work of Massine) and sought inspiration from natural movement and American subject matter.[21]

Loring and Copland were both well aware of the significance of finding a vernacular American style–a pursuit which occupied American artists of all disciplines in the 1930's. During the Depression, the principal national issues were social and financial ones. Many artists, disenchanted with a failed economic system, were attracted to leftist causes. They were spurred on by prestigious New York critics such as Olin Downes, who felt

---

[20]Loring discusses the reason for the March as a framing device, and the slight variation of its recapitulation, in his interview with Marilyn Hunt, 36-37.

[21]Philip 39.

that the Depression presented an opportunity for Americans to unlearn European traditions and find their own voice.[22] Said critic Roy D. Welch:

> a radical change has occurred in the relationship between musician and society....in human life and human society, nothing survives that is not truly functional, that is not seen to have a necessary part in the business of life.[23]

Proletarianism and the folk element in all forms of art became politically fashionable by the mid-1930's. The aftereffects of McCarthyism have largely hidden the extent and relative openness of the Leftist component in American arts and letters, and its profound influence on all the arts in the decade preceding the Second World War.[24]

Along with many other lesser known composers, Aaron Copland was an active participant in this movement. Trained in the austere, dissonant, internationalist style of post-World War I Europe, Copland by the mid 1930's was seeking to find a viable style to express the new Americanist spirit in his music. Indeed, *Billy* marks the advent of Copland's most accessible, populist period as a composer; it was followed by such quintessentially Americanist works as *Quiet City* (1939), *Of Mice and Men* (1939), *Our Town* (1940), *Lincoln Portrait* (1942), *Rodeo* (1942), *Fanfare for the Common Man* (1943), and *Appalachian Spring* (1944) – almost all of them collaborative works for film, theatre or ballet.

Loring, though not as politically active as Copland, was also interested in developing an accessible style, based on natural, meaningful movement, and expressing themes and issues concerning the rights of man.[25] In

---

[22]Olin Downes, "Music in the Changing Social Order – The Viewpoint of a Critic," *National Federation of Music Clubs: Book of Proceedings, 1933-1935*, ed. by Hazel G. Weaver (Ithaca, N.Y.: National Federation of Music Clubs, 1935)16.

[23]Roy Dickinson Welch, "The Musician and Society," *M.T.N.A. Proceedings, 1935* : 75.

[24]For a comprehensive analysis of the Americanist movement in music, see Barbara Zuck, *A History of Musical Americanism* (Ann Arbor: UMI Research Press, 1980); additional information can be found in H. Wiley Hitchcock, *Music in the United States: A Historical Introduction* , 3rd edition (Englewood Cliffs: Prentice-Hall, 1988) 199-209.

[25]Olga Maynard, "Eugene Loring Talks to Olga Maynard," *Dance Magazine* July 1966: 36.

response to a suggestion that one need not be American to choreograph an American-themed ballet, Loring responded:

> then how do you explain that Massine's *The New Yorker,* *Saratoga,* and *Union Pacific,* for all their themes drawn from American history, are positively not "American ballets" – and audiences and critics recognized that right from the start – while *Billy the Kid*...(is) as positively American...as Agnes de Mille's *Rodeo* and Jerome Robbin's *Fancy Free* ?[26]

This is the secret underlying *Billy's* initial success, and its subsequent and enduring popularity. Philosophically, the intent of both composer and choreographer was identical: to create a populist myth from a story of an American folk hero in a manner that was both accessible and in some way stylistically appropriate to that myth, and to elevate it to the level of art. American artists have been striving to duplicate that ideal ever since in their treatment of American heroes, historical figures, and events, from Agnes DeMille's *Rodeo* and Martha Graham's *Appalachian Spring* to Philip Glass' *The Photographer* and John Adams' *Nixon in China.*

---

[26]Maynard, *Dance Magazine* July 1966: 37-8.

THE GREEN TABLE

Choreography by Kurt Jooss

Score by Fritz Cohen

The Green Table, an expressionist ballet in eight scenes by German choreographer Kurt Jooss, received its premiere at the Theatre de la Champs Elysees in Paris on July 3, 1932. Subtitled a "Dance of Death," the work depicts the cynicism and deceit which lead to war, and its tragic results, in a series of eight related scenes with recurring characters.

Jooss was a student of the influential movement theorist Rudolph von Laban, and like Laban he sought more expressive choreographic alternatives to the traditional balletic style. *The Green Table* was Jooss's first major work, yet its significance was immediately recognized, and it is remembered today as a late-expressionist masterpiece of stylized movement function, archetypal characterizations of intense and pithy communicativeness, and sharply focused didacticism.[1]

Unfortunately, perhaps inevitably, *The Green Table* was never equalled. Jooss was forced to leave Germany because of his refusal to

---

[1]Marcia Siegel designates *The Green Table* as "late-expressionist" in style and dance idiom ("*The Green Table* – sources of a classic," *Dance Research Journal* 21.1 [1989]:15); but Hedwig Muller points out that "Kurt Jooss' 'expressionist' period slowly came to an end with his departure from the Tanzbuhne Laban...in 1924. In any case he had never really been an enthusiastic supporter of expressionism....He himself...did not wish to identify with the movement, his ideas were too far removed from impassioned zeal and were closer to a more pragmatic concept of dance and art in general." ("Jooss and Expressionism," *Jooss: Documentation by Anna and Hermann Markard* [Cologne: Ballet-Buhnen-Verlag, 1985] 13.)

dismiss his company's Jewish music director (and the composer of *The Green Table's* score), Frederic (Fritz) Cohen. Jooss spent most of the remainder of his career in England, and *The Green Table* stands alone among his works in terms of its popular impact and critical acclaim.

It is, ironically, the unique circumstances surrounding its creation that make *The Green Table's* themes so resonantly universal. The fateful confluence of time, place, and cultural fashion – prewar Germany, talented and socially concerned artists, and the development of the mature expressionist style – have produced a work which, while commenting so passionately on its time, consciously transcends its origins to express universal human feelings, a primary goal of expressionistic art.

The Green Table introduces us to archetypal characters whose emotions, characteristics, and actions are immediately and universally recognizable: the Young Soldier, the Woman, the Mother, the Profiteer, Death. Each character's movement vocabulary is very restricted and prescriptive, serving a highly denotative function. Death, the overseer of all the ballet's interior movements, is the most stylized of all: his choreography is placed predominately on the vertical axis, his upper body movements are large, deliberate and virile, and his repeated, steady foot stamps create an air of implacable and chilling inevitability, like Fate knocking at the door.[2] Other characters' movements also evoke perfectly the essence of their archetypal schema: the pliant, pleading arm gestures of the Young Woman, the wooden march of the Soldier, the crafty, indirect, ratlike gestures of the Profiteer, the mockingly belligerent poses of the diplomats.[3]

Fritz Cohen's two-piano score brilliantly parallels Jooss's combination of parody and pathos. According to Coton,

> Frederick Cohen worked as concentratedly upon the special musical problems of the Jooss ballets as their creator did on the choreographic problems. He saw the necessity for "thinking music" in the same way that the choreographer was

---

[2] For a more detailed discussion of Jooss's influences in the creation of the character of Death, see Siegel 16-18.

[3] A detailed discussion of these archetypal movement vocabularies may be found in Siegel 20-21.

"thinking dancing"... Choreographer and composer must between them effect absolute agreement of choreographic and musical forms.[4]

The music, utilizing a combination of social dance parodies, a heavy, rhythmic, folkish style, and some moments of relative dissonance, operates on several different levels:

- The dances satirize the sound and style of *fin-de-siecle* Viennese salon piano music, with its mock-civilized, almost banal ambience and bourgeois implications. In the ballet's framing scenes, involving the effete court dance of diplomacy, and in the Brothel scene, the composer uses these qualities to devastatingly ironic effect. To a Depression-era German audience, using such music in this context must have evoked a memory of a then-recent past rife with ethical lassitude, hyprocrisy, and moral decay – much like their own time.

- Contrarily, the score at other moments provided the honest simplicity, dynamic strength, and stylistic anonymity needed for those scenes which concern sincere human emotions. In these scenes, such as "The Farewell," "The Refugees" and "The Partisan," Cohen provides simple, modal, seemingly folk-influenced music to accompany the action. The inherent simplicity of a two-piano score, rather than orchestral accompaniment, renders these characters and situations more immediate and truthful, muting their inherent pathos somewhat.

- The occasional moments of dissonance are used at points of greatest conflict, such as "The Battle," or as dramatic foreshadowing, such as the measures immediately preceding the diplomats' gunshots.

- Ostinato is used most effectively in conjunction with the appearance of Death, underscoring his implacable, regular and horrific march.

Extended archetypal and emotional/psychological relationships in score and movement are both overwhelmingly evident throughout *The Green Table*; indeed, they represent an *urlinie* of choreomusical association which is everpresent. For this very reason, these relationships insinuate themselves slyly, at an almost subliminal perceptual level, and the ballet's passionate antiwar message is made all the more clear through this synergistic union of

---

[4]A. V. Coton, "Summary of the Achievement," *The New Ballet-Kurt Jooss and His Work* (London: Dennis Dobson, 1946) 78.

disciplines. The march of Death; the battle; the brothel; the aftermath; the diplomats – all are carefully presented by both composer and choreographer as universal characters and situations.

The Green Table opens with a brief, dirgelike musical introduction before the curtain rises, leaving us with little doubt as to the underlying emotional intent of the work. The first image is revealed: two opposed groups of diplomats are frozen in the act of negotiation across a large green table. Masks hide their faces. They wear evening coats, white gloves, and spats, the uniforms of supercilious civility. Periodically they change their poses, exploding into the stage space in a flurry of outstretched arms or extended legs.

Photo: Herbert Migdoll

The diplomats

170

Cohen provides a tango of exquisite banality and archness, belying the barely concealed malice of the diplomats. Its innocuous, square phrasing and falling melodic contour underscore the biting satire.

Fig. 1: Tango

The tango was then a popular social dance. Originating in Argentina, it was a love duet performed by couples in tight embrace, characterized by violent, erotic movement and abrupt rhythmic and dynamic contrasts. Tango texts were often very negative in tone, and the music was frequently in the minor mode.[5] These fruitless diplomatic posturings, through associative musical inference, assume the form of an amorous love duet, with death supplanting consummation as the ultimate goal of the game.

Here as elsewhere in *The Green Table*, there are pronounced rhythmic, dynamic and textural relationships between music and movement. Emphatic movement gestures such as outstretched arms or jumps occur on the tango's strong downbeats. Sometimes the dancers even make audible sounds to accompany the tango's characteristic rhythmic accent, such as hand

---

[5]"Tango," *The New Harvard Dictionary of Music,* 1986 ed.

slaps on the table. This curious form of movement-score integration becomes an increasingly important element of *The Green Table* in later scenes. (Unlike mimetic conceit, movement-score integration does not involve mimetic sound-making action, with the score providing the appropriate sound. Instead, the relationship is a purely rhythmic correspondence: the dancers make the sound themselves, and the result – a hand clap, foot stomp, etc. – becomes a planned and integrated component of the score.)

Cohen utilizes a loose rondo form for his tango, contrasting the almost idiotically cheery first theme in a major mode with episodes of increasing urgency and dissonance in the minor mode. During these turgid episodes, violent movements predominate. Leaps, belligerent solo grandstanding, and other pseudo-threatening behavior erupts between the two groups. But always the music returns to its "soothing" first theme, and we begin to perceive both the predictibility and insincerity of these little outbursts. We know that this conflict will continue indefinitely and that the diplomats have no intention of solving their dispute – too much enthusiasm is shown in the rituals of disagreement.

The gestures of the diplomats are consistent and tightly controlled. Their vocabulary is highly mimetic, strictly reinforcing the archetypal image. Individually, their gestures are unbalanced, unpredictable, constantly shifting. Yet the larger movement phrases are carefully phrased, logical, and often symmetrical.

Cohen provides us with some musical foreshadowing in this scene. During the diplomats' mock fights in the contrasting episodes of the rondo, we hear slightly disguised versions of themes from later scenes: the Farewell March (measures 53 and 54) and the Battle (measures 55 and 56).

Fig. 2

Their appearances here, though, are fleeting and quickly disintegrate into the first theme, suggesting that the diplomats are not at all serious about doing the fighting themselves.

The diplomats' final gesture confirms this suspicion. They draw guns, first pointing them at each other; then, after courtly bows, they fire the guns into the air on the final downbeat of the music—another example of movement-score integration. It is an act of both guilt and absolution. Starter pistol-style, they announce the beginning of the war. At the same time, they indicate their own unwillingness to fight. This final image is preceded in the score by chromatic chordal runs in contrary motion, a dissonant motive which is used repeatedly as a *leitmotif* to announce the arrival of points of particular crisis or impact.

Fig. 3

A brief transition section introduces us to the character of Death. Large, grotesque and menacing, he marches inexorably to the insistent, arpeggiated ostinato of a new musical accompaniment. We hear more pronounced dissonances: an obvious, reiterated tritone in the melody played loudly in octaves, for example. Like the music, Death's movements are all heavy, regular and stolid – a clear rhythmic relationship. Significantly, Cohen does not establish a thematic (i.e., recurring) parallel between the music and Death's appearances; as Death appears in each scene he always adjusts to the emotional and musical tenor of his surroundings, usually persuading or deceiving each character (except, as we shall see, in the case of the Profiteer) to cooperate with him. Without a characteristic, identifying theme, Death thus sneaks up on the audience as well.

Death   Photo: Herbert Migdoll

In "The Farewells," the marching motive which Death has established controls the pace of events. Cohen precedes this section with an ominous silence, broken only with intermittent, sharp octaves in the piano. Death stands upstage, sentinel-like, for a few seconds before beginning his march, a slow, repetitive pattern of foot stomping and walking. Death remains visible, like an inexorable metronome, as the Flag Bearer appears.

The Flag Bearer   Photo: Herbert Migdoll

This section contains another example of movement-score integration. The Flag Bearer uses his flag as a percussive instrument, drawing it quickly from side to side to accentuate beats one and three of every measure, the accented beats in this 4/4 march. After the Flag Bearer's bravura introduction, the tempo slows slightly and a second musical theme is introduced.

Fig. 4: Farewell March

The Flag Bearer becomes a drill sergeant as soldiers march onto the stage, echoing Death's own swinging arm movements. As the soldiers march through a stilted unison phrase, Cohen heavily reiterates the new theme by scoring it in octaves for both pianos. This is a common characteristic of the composer's thematic approach: themes are emphatically associated with moods and settings as much as they are with characters. These themes, once their associative function has been established, are reintroduced, often in varied forms, at times in the narrative when we are meant to infer relationships between different events (for example, the foreshadowing of the Battle theme in the opening diplomats' section).

At the entrance of the Young Girl, a much more lyrical and pensive musical theme is presented. The march tempo is maintained; however, the new theme breaks its rhythmic harshness with a soft but insistent quarter-note triplet counterrhythm in the melody.

The first theme returns with the entrance of the Profiteer. This character is unique in several important respects. He alone has a special relationship with Death: he is allowed to live. He reappears in scene after scene, usually at the end, to reap his rewards. Like the equally evil diplomats, he is dressed formally, in gloves, hat and spats. Like Death, at each appearance he alters the music in some way. Here, he ushers in the original marching theme – appropriate, since he has an obvious vested interest in this conflict. At the end of "The Farewells," after the soldiers march off to war, the Profiteer bows to Death in gratitude.

At the end of "The Farewells" we hear another example of musical foreshadowing: the small, falling phrase presages the battle motive, which follows.

The theme of "The Battle," in agitated 3/2 time, consists of two short motivic phrases in sequence over a jangling, high-tessitura, arpeggiated ostinato.

Fig. 5: The Battle

The slow half-note beat unit is needed for the large throws and jumps which the fight entails. We see in the soldiers' strident fighting movement the violent and literal enhancement of the diplomats' earlier gestures. Mere spars and feints are now the veritable thrusts and parries of bayonet and sword. The centerpiece of this scene is the flag wrestling duet, accompanied by a single, homorhythmic theme in octaves. We hear strong instances of bitonality here, in the opposed *fortissimo* triadic chords played alternately by the two pianos. Although this is an appropriate musical conceit, "The Battle" in general suffers from an absence of greater dissonance – in keeping with Cohen's prevailing musical language for the ballet as a whole, but a weakness, perhaps, in comparison with the strength and tension of the choreography.

The choreography for "The Battle" is appropriately violent, but it is also carefully structured, frequently in unison, quite symmetrical, and non-developmental. After the flag duo the combatants proceed as before, and at the end there is no clear victor. The battle is brought to an abrupt halt only with Death's reappearance (throughout *The Green Table*, Death is the only character with the power to freeze musical and choreographic events). He proceeds to march slowly and stiffly through the body-strewn battlefield to a slow $\frac{3}{4}$ variation of the "Battle" theme – the ultimate victor on parade. As he exits, the Profiteer reappears to pick the pockets of the victims. We hear a recapitulation of the warrior's duet theme as he dances a macabre, ferretlike victory jig over the bodies.

Fig. 6: Profiteer's Theme

Here the Profiteer's movement characteristics – quick, furtive, multi-directional – become more clearly established. He exits, gloating over his booty, to a ghostly echo of the Battle theme.

"The Refugees" introduces us to the first adagio of the ballet. The music is a slow, ululative $\frac{12}{8}$, modal and sad.

Fig. 7: The Refugees' Theme

Group movements consist largely of slowly changing tableaux. The movements of the Old Woman – she darts forward, only to be pulled backward by unseen hands again and again – echo the rising and falling left-hand motive in the accompaniment. She is constantly bent backward and forward through the vertical axis – Death's axis. This is the score's quietest, most pensive moment. The theme continues in simple variation form as the women's group slowly advances in a downstage right diagonal direction.

Death's appearance downstage right again stops the phrase-flow of the music and action temporarily. Recommencing, the theme becomes fragmented; then, assuming its original form, it modulates upward. The women scatter. Death calls gently yet insistently to the Old Woman, drawing her to him. As he picks her up and carries her off, the theme reaches a gentle climax, but without the angst or terror heard during the battle of the previous scene. Death simultaneously controls and adapts to the choreomusical environment of each scene he enters, changing it only subtly as he performs his grim task. The Profiteer's brief appearance after Death's exit also alters the music, agitating it into a louder dynamic, before he struts slowly offstage.

The Partisan enters stridently with a long and loping gait, waving a scarf. Her entrance is an obvious imitation of the battle scene's flag bearer. The music is martial, repetitive and modal, like a folk anthem.

The Partisan   Photo: Herbert Migdoll

Fig. 8: The Partisan's Theme

Her movement consists of rapid turns, outwardly flung arms, and jumps.

The music changes meter from $\frac{6}{8}$ to a brisk $\frac{2}{4}$ march step, and soldiers enter, marching from upstage left to upstage right. At their second entrance she strikes one with her scarf, killing him. Surrounded, she is approached by Death; a dirge-like death march is heard and she is led by Death, as a member of a firing squad, slowly downstage left. Death plays the role of the executioner, signalling the firing squad to kill her. At the moment of her death, an old theme reappears: the chromatic octaves in contrary motion, last heard at the end of the first scene, just before the diplomats fire their guns into the air. This time, though, the theme is inverted, falling instead of rising in pitch. As she dies at Death's feet, the final chord of the cadence is soft, major, and almost ethereally peaceful.

Fig. 9: chromatic sequence

"The Brothel" introduces a second bitterly satirical social dance form, the waltz. Like the first scene's tango, its characteristics are overemphasized and made grotesque in order to underscore the biting irony of the scene.

Fig. 10: Waltz

The waltz, of course, was the very popular and elegant social dance of nineteenth-century court and salon. Originating in what is now southern Germany and Austria, the waltz transformed from a country dance of rather questionable and salacious character into a ballroom dance of the utmost grace, elegance and sophistication by the end of the eighteenth century. The Viennese waltz, with its pronounced agogic accent and distinctive rubato, was perhaps the best-known social dance form of the late nineteenth and early twentieth centuries.[6]

Cohen's and Jooss' waltz is a travesty of the form. Brazenly chromatic, weighted down by egregiously overemphasized agogic accents, the music is a masterpiece of bombast, skewing all the elegant Viennese waltz conventions and niceties to the point of grotesqueness. The Profiteer relishes his role as a macabre Master of Ceremonies, controlling the Young Girl's movements and her choice of partners. She stares blankly ahead, almost catatonic, before being pulled into the lustful, swirling dance, an unwilling but helpless pawn in the Profiteer's game. She is thrust from soldier to soldier, manipulated like a rag doll, and perfunctorily raped. With a clap of his hands, the Profiteer initiates a multi-partnered reprise of this macabre dance.

The waltz dissolves quickly as Death enters. His approach from upstage left is disguised – he is behind the Young Girl's lover (a mirage, perhaps?), approaching with outstretched arms. But it is a cruel joke. The boy walks blindly by, and Death takes possession of her, indulging in the final rape to a frightening, hugely augmented version of the waltz's second theme. He lulls her tenderly into death – a welcome respite – seeming to feed like a vampire on her body as the music cadences and fades in a blissful major mode.

---

[6]"Waltz," *The New Harvard Dictionary of Music*, 1986 ed.

"The Aftermath" begins as a processional.

Fig. 11: Aftermath Theme

To tender and quiet introductory chords, Death slowly takes the flag from the Flag Bearer and leads the slow marchers downstage left. The "Farewell" theme is then recapitulated, greatly augmented, in doubled octaves.

188

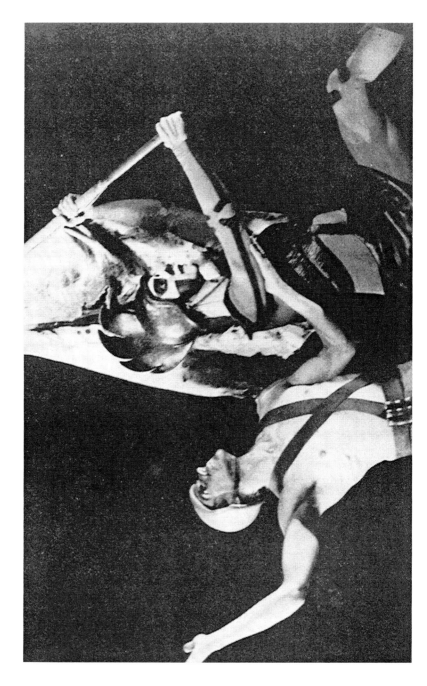

Photo: Herbert Migdoll

Death leads the Flag Bearer

Each character retains some semblance of his or her own individualized movement vocabulary, despite marching in lockstep. All the figures, though, are constantly pulled into verticality (Death's axis), jerking like puppets as they do so to a pronounced, dry eighth-note triplet figure in the score. Death's flag acts like a scythe as he mows all the characters down in a sweeping arc. Each character meets the same fate; even the crafty Profiteer (who enters at the end of the scene, marked by discordant jangles in the music) cannot escape Death, though he struggles more than the others and is less accepting of his fate. Death must actually work a bit to ensnare the Profiteer. The music resorts to the terrifying ostinato theme with which he was first introduced (the only other time this music is heard), and it is transformed into a confusing $\frac{6}{4}$ meter as he finally defeats the Profiteer – musical evidence, perhaps, that he is Death's only real, if momentary, challenge.

Loud contrary motion chords lead us into the final scene, just as contrary motion brought us out of the first scene, and a sharp gunshot thrusts us back into the initial tableau freeze of *The Green Table*: the bickering diplomats. Cleverly, Jooss has us rejoin them at the instant we left them – the moment of the gunshot – and nothing has changed. Their ritualistic feints and apologies, abbreviated somewhat in the recapitulation, seem doubly ironic. If anything, the movement is even more stylized, the music even more arch and mock-playful. We are left with a sense of profound futility.

The strength of *The Green Table's* choreomusical constructs lies in their complete and synergistic devotion to the theme of the work, at the expense of virtuosity, structural complexity, and other artistic conceits. Every note and movement is dedicated to the conveyance of *The Green Table's* message: "war is ugly, useless – and inevitable."[7] In the collaborations of Stravinsky and Balanchine, there is more room for compositional and choreographic virtuosity, for the personalities of the performers to influence the work, for variations of musical interpretation by conductor and orchestra. These are all necessary (or at least expected) adjuncts of performance.

---

[7]Marcia Siegel, "*The Green Table*: Movement Masterpiece," *At the Vanishing Point* (New York: Saturday Review Press, 1972) 61.

Not so with *The Green Table*. There are very good reasons why the performance of this work has been so tightly controlled by Jooss's disciples over the years.[8] With Laban's guidance, Jooss had painstakingly developed a new movement language whose every small detail was not only tightly controlled, but imbued with vital communicative significance. Such a language leaves little room for the nuances of individual interpretation. The dancers are expected to completely sublimate their technique to the greater purpose of expressing the meaning of the work.[9] Siegel notes that Jooss believed "all movement has an expressive as well as a functional content, and that the qualities inherent in movement can be taken as a direct statement of feeling."[10] As well, Siegel and others have observed that Jooss has deliberately and carefully chosen only those movement qualities which reinforce the dramatic content of the ballet.[11]

Both Jooss and Cohen also share a keen sense of satire and irony. Each was well aware of the intrinsic affective power of familiar things: a waltz step, for example, or white gloves, tails and spats. These and other icons of popular culture are used by composer and choreographer in identical ways, as the tools of satire – the sharp instruments that allowed them to scratch the thin veneer of a volatile European culture in crisis and expose the horror underneath.

---

[8] All aspects of *The Green Table's* performance are carefully prescribed by the executors of the Kurt Jooss estate.

[9] See Fernau Hall, "An Interview with Kurt Jooss", *Dancing Times* November 1945:56. It should be noted, however, that improvisation was an important element of Jooss's choreographic process, and he drew frequently from his own dancers' interpretations of his own movement. See "The Value of Jooss," Coton 71-76.

[10] Siegel, *Vanishing Point* 63.

[11] Siegel, *Vanishing Point* 63.

ERRAND INTO THE MAZE

Choreography by Martha Graham
Score by Gian Carlo Menotti

Errand into the Maze is an analysis of fear. Inspired, says the choreographer, by a terrifying and nearly disastrous airplane ride over the mountains of Iran, it is her choreographic response to the experience.[1] The source of fear is not made explicit in the work, though it is embodied, powerfully and graphically, by a strong and menacing male figure. The protaganist of the work is a woman, originally danced by Graham herself. With sets by Isamu Noguchi and music by Gian Carlo Menotti, *Errand into the Maze* received its premiere on April 28, 1947.

The work opens on a stage with the barest of set pieces: a large, V-shaped sculpture stage left, suggesting a bone or perhaps horns. A thin white thread leads in a zig-zag fashion from the sculpture to a small upstage cube. A rope extends diagonally from the cube into the flies. Two suspended objects suggest a surrealistic moon and star. The setting is metaphysical, stark, and foreboding.

---

[1]*An evening of dance and conversation with Martha Graham*, Dance in America series, WNET/Thirteen, New York, 1984.

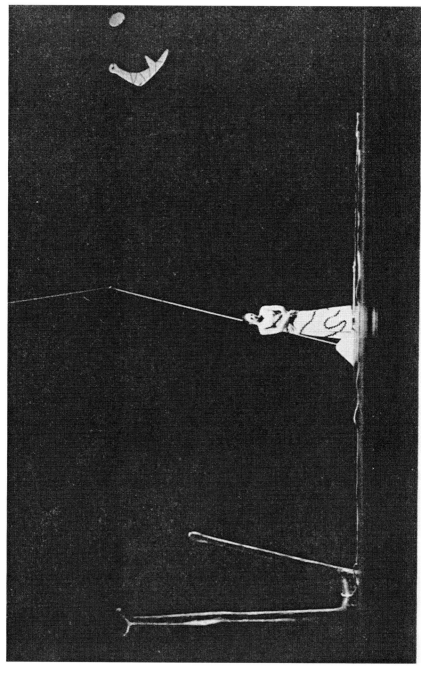

Photo: Martha Swope

Set of *Errand Into the Maze*

A woman stands near the cube, in a state of rising apprehension. She is obviously troubled by some inner conflict; she is constantly racked by small contractions and furtive, nervous movements of the head and upper body. She follows the path of the rope quickly to the horn sculpture, dances a brief solo, then comes back to the horns, feeling them as if they afford her some comfort or protection.

A Minotaur-like beast enters. Slowly, steadily, with excruciating patience, it pursues the woman.

Minotaur behind Ariadne   Photo: Martha Swope

The beast is prevented from touching her, however, by a rodlike yoke which keeps its arms pinned high and behind its torso in a menacing yet impotent stance. Finally, the woman manages to push the Minotaur offstage.

During the following interlude, some residual tension remains in music and movement. The woman dances in front of the rope, then gathers it up through the V-shaped opening of the horns. She quickly constructs a net with the rope, fashioning it slingshot-style around the horns. She finishes it just as the Minotaur enters for a second time.

Ariadne constructs her net

Photo: Martha Swope

This time the conflict is even more ominous and menacing. The beast slowly and inexorably dominates the woman, eventually standing over her prone body, stepping over her from side to side as she rolls away from it. Finally she is spun violently around by the arms. After escaping its grip, the woman manages somehow to push it offstage.

The woman's second solo interlude is calmer than the first. Still, some underlying tension peeks through the prevailingly lyrical phrases in score and choreography. Small contractions creep into her movement vocabulary as the music becomes more strident and rhythmic. The Minotaur springs energetically into view, its most frightening entrance yet. The music is an oppressively heavy $\frac{6}{8}$. Continuing to hop, the beast threatens her from behind. This time, though, she challenges it more physically than in the previous encounters. She hops onto the Minotaur's bent legs, facing it in a brute struggle for the only time. The beast collapses.

In the final solo interlude, the woman travels upstage to the horns and takes down her rope barrier to calm and cadential music. She feels the horns tenderly, lovingly as the lights dim and her figure becomes a silhouette.

Ariadne removes the net   Photo: Martha Swope

Errand into the Maze is based on the ancient Greek myth of Theseus and the Minotaur. Half man and half bull, the Minotaur was the product of a bestial union between Pasiphae, wife of Cretan king Minos, and a bull. The beast was banished by Minos to spend its life hidden in a vast maze. It was fed every nine years on the blood of Athenian youths and maidens. Volunteering on one such sacrificial occasion, Theseus, son of the Athenian king Aegeus, entered the labyrinth and slew the Minotaur. He was able to find his way out of the Minotaur's lair by following a thread which he had unwound, given to him by Ariadne, daughter of Minos.

The myth of the Minotaur has proven to be an enduringly popular one in Western art, and among Graham's contemporaries and immediate predecessors the Minotaur-influenced works of Matisse, Cocteau, and especially Picasso are considered important. Picasso was able to integrate both mythological and Spanish folk elements in his depictions of the Minotaur, and in his art it is often an image of immense strength, virility, and eroticism, not necessarily an evil force.

Other details of the story reverberate in strange and interesting ways throughout the imagery of Western culture. The maze, for example, has become a pervasive concept, appearing even in folk dance:

> ...the labyrinth...recalls the mazes marked out as ritual dancing patterns in many countries from Wales to northeast Russia, always in connection with a cavern.[2]

The use of a thread, rope or other marker to negotiate a maze or other obstacle is also a recurrent theme in Western folklore and literature. Most people are familiar with such episodes in familiar childhood stories: the fairy tales of Sleeping Beauty and Hansel and Gretel, for example, or Lewis Carroll's *Through the Looking Glass*.

It is probable that Graham's female protaganist is, in fact, Ariadne. The choreographer has given us some clues. In Ovid's description of the myth, the well-meaning Ariadne, though she provides Theseus with his means of escape, is rewarded for her deed with tragedy and despair. She leaves her family to be with Theseus, but he cruelly abandons her and returns

---

[2]Michael Grant, *Myths of the Greeks and Romans* (New York: Mentor, 1962) 341.

alone to Athens.[3] Notice the similarities at this point in the story between the myth and Graham's adaptation of it. After her abandonment, Ariadne

> wandered distractedly along the beach...crying out to her faithless lover, she desperately asked what would become of her. But as she wept, there was suddenly a sound of cymbals and frenzied drumbeats, and she was afraid...three times she tried to flee [from the amorous advances of Dionysus] but could not...and they departed together.[4]

These details were freely adapted by Graham, and their context has changed radically. Graham is always more interested in portraying women as protaganists, not as victimized and manipulated pawns (as in the myth) but as masters of their own fate. To Graham, "a traditional feminine stance can be adopted only as a weapon or as a sign of weakness. She seldom found a way for men and women to be equals."[5] In giving to Ariadne the role of Theseus, Graham redefines her place in the mythological hierarchy from passive to active protaganist by altering the nuances of the mythological details she retains. Graham's Ariadne is made fearful of the drumbeats only initially; gradually they become the means to her empowerment, a call to arms. Graham's Ariadne doesn't make three ultimately futile attempts to flee an amorous male god, but three ultimately successful attempts to defeat a defiant and frightening male enemy. The Ariadne of *Errand* uses the thread not as an escape from the monster's lair, but as a path to it – she actively seeks the heart of her fear, and even though it is well concealed, she must confront it. Indeed, a sinuous version of the string is embroidered into her very costume, passing over her own heart. She defeats the Minotaur not with a show of forceful physical superiority, but by facing him down and revealing the underlying powerlessness of his masculine aggressiveness. She is in every

---

[3]Various sources differ regarding Ariadne's fate after her abandonment. Homer maintains she was killed by Dionysus; other sources claim she committed suicide. Later writers even indulge in speculative and demeaning explanations, such as Boccaccio's theory (in his *Genealogia decorum*) that Ariadne was drunk.

[4]Grant 341-42.

[5]Marcia Siegel, "The Harsh and Splendid Heroines of Martha Graham, "*Watching the Dance Go By* (Boston: Houghton Mifflin, 1977) 205.

sense a modern woman, and *Errand* can be viewed as a triumphant feminist statement.

Graham may have borrowed freely from other details of the myth as well. Theseus was said to have celebrated his victory over the Minotaur with the Athenian youths in a dance known as the *Geranos* or Crane Dance. Performed around an altar, the dance patterns mimicked the twists and turns of the labyrinth. The altar itself, called a *keraton*, was composed of animal horns. We can see the influence of these elements in both Graham's choreography and Noguchi's spare, animalistic sculpture.

The choreomusical relationship of greatest significance in *Errand* is emotional/psychological parallel, and neither movement nor music sways from its relentless course of the portrayal of combatting one's fears. This conflict is depicted as a recurring battle with three distinct levels:

> – **Fear**. Ariadne is racked with apprehension of the conflict to come. This level is characterized by her small, violent contractions and jerks of the body, particularly the head, and small, often sidelong steps. The musical vocabulary features prominent percussion accents which usually initiate the contractions and twitches of Ariadne in sharp rhythmic parallel.

> – **Struggle**. Ariadne struggles with the Minotaur three times. Each fight, as we shall see, is attuned to a slightly different dynamic. The music becomes martial, increasingly dissonant, metrically rhythmic, and strident with each entrance of the Minotaur; loud French horn is usually prominently featured during his presence.

> – **Triumph**. Often characterized by regular, repeated movements and a more relaxed choreographic vocabulary, these solo sections for Ariadne succeed each struggle with the Minotaur. The music becomes much less dissonant, and woodwinds (particularly flute and oboe) are prominent.

To the extent that each of these choreomusical affinities recurs, the relationship could be labelled thematic, though the materials are not specific – no precise musical themes or clearly reiterated movement phrases can be identified. The correspondences are less literal, belonging more to a loose familial pattern of relationships than closely interwoven instances. We are left with constructive essences which seem intrinsically suited to each

202

other: the contraction, for example, the veritable mortar of Graham's choreographic materials, and its musical counterpart, the percussive accent.

    Errand opens with the sound of a disjunct and rhythmically irregular solo piano melody, a harbinger of things to come.

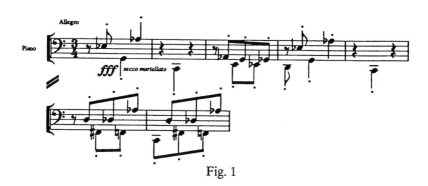

Fig. 1

Ariadne is wracked by small contractions and jerks of the head, all in precise rhythmic and dynamic parallel to the score. The first few minutes of the piece are rife with such relationships – for instance, the correspondence of her sudden head movements with sharp piano and percussion gestures.

Fig. 2

The exact rhythmic correspondence between percussive, often syncopated accents and sharp, small body movements breaks down somewhat as Ariadne begins to trace the sinuous line of the rope, acrobat-style, downstage left. Although the rhythmic accents roughly parallel her steps, the relationship is no longer a mirror-image one; now the percussive accents act as initiators of her halting, spurting movement.

Other more subtle relationships begin to make themselves felt. We hear a rather sinuous, undulating melodic line as Ariadne traces the tortuous, winding path of her rope.

Fig. 3

Fig. 3, *continued*

Also, rhythmic accents begin to initiate increasingly large movements. After Ariadne passes through the "portal" sculpture, small percussive accents act as the impetus for large leg swings. We notice, too, that structural parallels are not scrupulously maintained – the choreography plays through the music's moments of structural repose and phrase-end cadences, and the movement keeps its sharp, neurotic angularity even during those occasional moments when the music becomes more lyrical. There are metric disparities as well: dance and music frequently act counter-rhythmically to each other, such as during the brief flute solo in this opening section.

The score becomes noticeably more dissonant with the first entrance of the Minotaur. The meter transforms into a slow, strongly syncopated $\frac{3}{4}$ as he takes position behind her. Woodwinds dominate:

Fig. 4

The ponderousness of the rhythm is echoed by the awkwardness of their movement. There is a sense of unresolvedness and struggle in both music and movement in the scenes involving the Minotaur. Menotti is careful not only to introduce a higher level of dissonance, but to avoid any feeling of resolution or easing up in this section.

After the Minotaur's first exit, Ariadne dances a solo to a slightly softened version of his preceding entrance theme, as if she has absorbed some of his qualities. Then a new, almost tender theme in $\frac{6}{8}$ time acts as the impetus to propel her down the string a second time, noticeably faster than the first.

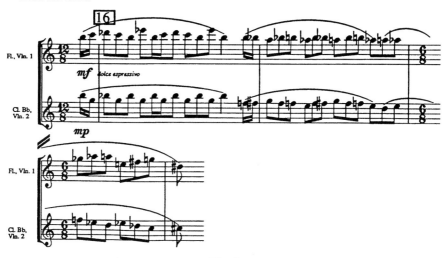

Fig. 5

As she gathers up the rope, the increasing tension in her movements is echoed by an ominous tremolo motive in the strings. Just before the Minotaur's second entrance we hear a martial, rising fifth horn motive, the clearest thematic association of brass instruments with the Minotaur up to this point.

Fig. 6

Graham occasionally provides us with curious, isolated mimetic conceits, such as the use of a rolled timpani here as the Minotaur, on its back, shakes its raised foot violently. The sound is a chilling demonstration of its power. Yet we begin to realize that the Minotaur, for all its menace and ferocity, is ultimately powerless to physically harm Ariadne. It can tyrannize her emotionally, but it never strikes her – the yoke prevents any arm movement. The Minotaur's underlying powerlessness is reflected, too, in Menotti's clever score. His musical accompaniment is powerful, harshly dissonant, yet its constantly rising tension never reaches the expected climax; it remains unresolved. The Minotaur generally moves to the slower beat unit in the musical texture – its gestures are much slower and more deliberate than those of Ariadne.

Graham, too, uses several devices to augment the level of tension during the Minotaur's appearances. At one point in its second appearance, it leaps over Ariadne twice, then hops on the unaccented beats of the heavy, threatening music. The result is very unsettling. Then both characters move precisely to rapid musical cues:

– Ariadne throws her head back on a sharp timpani accent;

– the Minotaur straddles Ariadne and turns its leg in and out quickly, in time with the short, repeated motive;

– the Minotaur lifts its arches sharply with every quick step it takes as the snare drum accents each step.

Other elements further heighten the tension:

– the strings reach an ever-higher tessitura as the scene progresses;

- the French horn returns at the climax of the scene, as the Minotaur swings Ariadne around itself.

All of these movements have a cumulatively threatening effect, even though they never result in overt violence. Through the use of these devices, dramatic tension is increased to an almost unbearable pitch each time the Minotaur challenges Ariadne.

Even in those episodes of relative calm between each conflict, Graham and Menotti are careful to maintain an almost subliminal subtext of tension. In the moments following the Minotaur's second exit, for example, the music is lighter, predominately major, and woodwind-dominated, typical of the "triumph" level. However, we can still detect subtle elements of tension in the score. Small repeated melodic cells and strange "hiccup" accents in the woodwinds, accompanied by small twitches and other forms of movement accent, assure us that though the battle may be over, the conflict has not yet been resolved.

Fig. 7

The return of an ostinato pattern in the percussion instruments presages the third entrance of the Minotaur. Ariadne's characteristic "fear" vocabulary of twitches and small contractions returns, each one initiated by a percussive accent in the score.

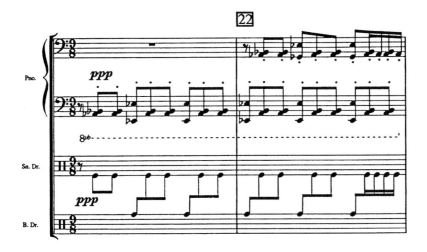

Fig. 8

But while this ostinato is the impetus for distressing and fearful movement motives in Ariadne, it seems to have an empowering effect on the Minotaur: it enters bouncing powerfully to the dotted-quarter beat unit, with a springlike, energetic and almost perverse energy. Though the music for this third and final struggle seems suitably martial, with strings and woodwinds antiphonally opposed and playing jagged, disjunct lines, there is little use of brass in this episode. Perhaps the composer is hinting that the Minotaur, for all its ostensible force-fulness (this is certainly its most menacing entrance so far), is losing some of its power. In this struggle, the point of greatest musical tension arrives at the choreography's most crucial point: the defeat of the Minotaur. There is a curious reversal of roles here as Ariadne stands over the supine Minotaur, in a pose very similar to its own from the previous conflict episode. The French horn is finally audible during the fortissimo cadence which accompanies its death. The music finally reaches its long-avoided resolution as the Minotaur turns over and expires.

210

In the final section, marked Lento, a sense of serene resolution is achieved. The instruments of triumph reappear: woodwinds, dominated by a long, lyrical oboe melody. The music is still linked subtly by time signature ($\frac{3}{4}$) to the previous struggle. Now, though, it has the effect of a calming, slow waltz. It is the only slow, lyrical moment in the entire work.

Fig. 9

After considering *Errand* in its entirety, several large-scale constructive elements become apparent:

> – rhythmic relationships between movement and music are at their closest and most apparent during "fear" sections. Graham's choreographic depiction of fear in this work, involving several sharp, small accented movements and contractions, are almost always motivated by percussive accents;

> – the use of orchestrational association as in archetypal relationship, while never scrupulously exact, is pervasive: French horn with Minotaur, fear with percussive accents, triumph with woodwinds;

> – dramatic tension is carefully maintained throughout the work until the very moment of the Minotaur's death. The only real cadence occurs with the final three chords, and even they are harmonically complex – not true resolutions in the traditional harmonic sense.

Surely the secret of *Errand's* success, and one of its most impressive qualities, is the elegance and succinct efficiency of its structure. It is a duet with a simple set; the theme is presented clearly and unaffectedly; three points of conflict build to a satisfying resolution; movement vocabulary is plain and understated.

Yet this simple and elegant work examines our deepest, most concealed fears: of death, of the unknown, of the beast in us. Only by reducing these fears to a tangible, recognizable form and confronting them, says Graham, can we live our lives as Ariadne lives hers when we leave her – purely, bravely, and unburdened of their weight.

CONCLUSION

At the beginning of this book, I warned that it would be difficult to analyze something as intrinsic and ineffable as the dance-music partnership, and indeed it has proven to be an often elusive subject, slipping out from under the microscope slide like some constantly mutating organism. In fact, the relationship between music and dance is Protean in nature, capable of changing its definition and significance from work to work, often used in completely different ways by each composer and choreographer which we have studied. The paradigm has proven to be only partially successful in identifying and describing the many meaningful connections, both overt and subtle, which permeate each great ballet – or, to be more accurate, it merely identifies those connections in broad, generic fashion, leaving us with the task of filling in the details in each case. Perhaps, some would argue, it is better to allow the partnership to exist without the need for self-conscious and overly intellectual analysis. Different artistic disciplines will naturally find interstices, and these correspondences are simply the incidental results of shared structural and aesthetic rules and/or tendencies, after all.

Even from a strictly analytical perspective, though, this attitude invites misconceptions. Truly collaborative art forms must be evaluated in their multidisciplinary entirety. To examine the choreography or score of a collaborative masterwork as a discrete and autonomous artistic statement is a grievous oversight – like watching a film in silence, or hearing an opera on the radio. This is exactly the premise of Irene Marion Alm's excellent structural analysis of the choreography and score of Stravinsky's and

Balanchine's *Agon*.[1] Previous analyses of the score alone, proves Alm, have been seriously flawed because of their failure to take into account both the choreography and the ballet's well-documented working out process, each of which is crucial to an understanding of *Agon's* structure. Clearly, the significance of one discipline cannot be discounted by scholars whose disciplinary education and allegiances lie with the other. The implications, I hope are clear: those scholars who analyze dance works, be they dance- or music-educated, must adopt a broader, cross-disciplinary approach, accepting music and dance as equal artistic partners, assuming that they act in synergy (rather than independence or even opposition) in any collaborative masterwork; and an examination of the collaborative process of a given work, a knowledge of the history of a collaborative partnership, and a familiarity with each artist's aesthetic approach are all essential to comprehensive analysis. Such knowledge would even help to explain, for example, the seemingly random sound-movement oppositions of a Cunningham-Cage collaboration as relationships of aesthetic philosophy and process.

Choreographers and composers, too, cannot afford to ignore the powerful and pervasive effects which each discipline exerts upon the other. Perhaps the most important creative discoveries to be gleaned from these analyses are that even oblique, covert relationships are ultimately readable at some perceptual level, and that the viewer's aural and visual perception are constantly influencing each other and coloring the overall effect of the work. Another notable characteristic of most of these ballets is the choreographers' studied avoidance of calculated or overly obvious choremusical relationships. When Balanchine, for example, created choreographic realizations of musical canons, he never attempted literal correspondences between dancers and instruments or parts. Instead, he looked for the essence of that music-movement relationship and reduced his choreographic response to the most economical vocabulary possible, giving us the spirit of that canon, not its virtual kinetic translation.

Intrinsic relationships were often layered or presented simultaneously in each of the six ballets, although, as noted, overt correspondences of

[1]Irene Alm, "Stravinsky, Balanchine, and Agon: An Analysis Based on the Collaborative Process," *The Journal of Musicology* 7.2 (Spring 1989) 254-269.

dynamic, texture, quality and especially rhythm were sometimes deliberately avoided. Intrinsic contrasts were used frequently, often as an element of surprise. The most effective extrinsic relationships were the result of strongly focused unity of purpose and theme. Choreographer and composer shared a perfectly matched vision – a psychological study of a Western outlaw, a passionate antiwar message – and developed aesthetically similar languages to achieve that vision.

The magic of the marriage of dance and music is due, in part, to the chimerical nature of the bonding and reinforcing process between them, and the feeling of synergy which results from their simultaneous performance – that the whole is indeed far greater than the sum of its parts. However, while the relationship is sometimes ineffable, it is by no means completely indefinable. By trying to understand choreomusical processes, becoming consciously rather than instinctively aware of their power, we can appreciate more readily the powerful force of dance and music intelligently weeded, perhaps even learn to use their allied power more effectively as creators and performers.

SELECTED BIBLIOGRAPHY

Alm, Irene Marion. "Stravinsky, Balanchine and *Agon*: The Collaborative Process." Diss. University of California, Los Angeles, 1985.

_____. "Stravinsky, Balanchine, and *Agon:* An Analysis Based on the Collaborative Process." *The Journal of Musicology* 7 (1989): 254-269.

Brent, Jonathan, Peter Gena and Don Gillespie, eds. *A Cage Reader.* New York: C. F. Peters, 1982.

Buckle, Richard and John Taras. *George Balanchine: Ballet Master.* London: Hamish Hamilton, 1988.

Butterworth, Neil. *The Music of Aaron Copland.* London: Toccata Press, 1985.

Cohen, F. A. "The Green Table." Unpublished manuscript for solo piano; arrangement of original two-piano version. New York: Dance Notation Bureau, n.d.

Cohen, Selma Jeanne, ed. *Dance as a Theatre Art: Source Reading in Dance History from 1581 to the Present.* New York: Harper & Row, 1974.

Cohen, Selma Jeanne and Herbert Read. *Stravinsky and the Dance.* New York: New York Public Library, 1962.

Coker, Wilson. *Music & Meaning: A Theoretical Introduction.* New York: The Free Press, 1972.

Copeland, Roger and Marshal Cohen, eds. *What is Dance?* Oxford: Oxford University Press, 1983.

Copland, Aaron. *Billy the Kid.* New York: Boosey & Hawkes, 1941.

_____. "Billy the Kid." 1938. Unpublished manuscript for two pianos. New York: Dance Notation Bureau, 1986.

Copland, Aaron and Vivian Perlis. *Copland: 1900 Through 1942.* New York: St. Martin's/Marek, 1982.

Coton, A. V. *The New Ballet-Kurt Jooss and His Work.* London: Dennis Dobson, Ltd., 1946.

Cowell, Henry, ed. *American Composers on American Music.* 2nd ed. New York: Ungar, 1962.

Craft, Robert, ed. *Stravinsky: Selected Correspondence*. 3 vols. New York: Alfred A. Knopf, 1982.

Danilova, Alexandra. "Danilova on Balanchine." *Dance Magazine* July 1983: 62.

Denby, Edwin. *Dancers Buildings and People in the Streets*. New York: Horizon, 1965.

_____. *Looking at the Dance*. New York: Pellegrini & Cudahy, 1943.

Ferguson, Donald. *Music as Metaphor: The Elements of Expression* . 1960. Westport: Greenwood Press, 1973.

Garis, Robert. "Balanchine-Stravinsky: Facts and Problems." *Ballet Review* 10.3 (1982): 9-23.

Grant, Michael. *Myths of the Greeks and Romans*. New York: Mentor, 1962.

Haggin, B. H. "Balanchine: Musician-Choreographer." *Dance Index* July 1942: 111-112.

_____. "Reflections on Balanchine." *Dance Magazine* July 1983: 56.

Hanslick, Eduard. *The Beautiful in Music* . 1854. Trans. Gustav Cohen. 7th ed. New York: The Liberal Arts Press, 1957.

Hastings, Baird. *Choreographer and Composer*. Boston: Twayne, 1983.

Hitchcock, H. Wiley. *Music in the United States: A Historical Introduction*. 3rd ed. Englewood Cliffs: Prentice Hall, 1988.

Horst, Louis and Carol Russell. *Modern Dance Forms in Relation to the other Modern Arts*. San Francisco: Impulse Publications, 1961.

Horst, Louis. *Pre-Classic Dance Forms*. 1937. New York: Dance Horizons, 1979.

Humphrey, Doris. *The Art of Making Dances*. New York: Rinehart & Co., 1959.

Jaques-Dalcroze, Emile. *Rhythm, Music and Education*. Trans. Harold F. Rubinstein. 3rd ed. New York: G. P. Putnam's Sons, 1931.

Katz, Ruth and Carl Dalhaus, eds. *Contemplating Music: Source Readings in the Aesthetics of Music*. Vol 1. New York: Pendragon Press, 1987.

Kirstein, Lincoln. "About Billy the Kid." *The Dance Observer* October 1938: 116.

Kivy, Peter. *The Corded Shell: Reflections on Musical Expression.* Princeton: Princeton University Press, 1980.

_____. *Sound and Semblance: Reflections on Musical Representation.*

_____. Princeton: Princeton University Press, 1984.

Kostelanetz, Richard. *Conversing with Cage.* New York: Limelight, 1988.

LaFave, Kenneth. "Point Counterpoint." *Ballet News* June 1983: 22-26.

Langer, Susanne K. *Problems of Art.* New York: Charles Scribner's Sons, 1957.

Lassalle, Nancy, ed. "Stravinsky and Balanchine: Fifty Years of Partnership: 1920-1971." Souvenir program, New York City Ballet, 1971.

Lederman, Minna, ed. *Stravinsky in the Theatre.* 1949. New York: Da Capo, 1975.

Levy, Alan Howard. *Musical Nationalism: American Composers' Search for Identity.* Westport: Greenwood Press, 1983.

Loring, Eugene. Interview with Marilyn Hunt. New York City Public Library, Lincoln Center Dance Collection, 1976.

Maynard, Olga. *The American Ballet.* Philadelphia: Macrae Smith, 1959.

_____. "Balanchine and Stravinsky: The Glorious Undertaking." *Dance Magazine* June 1972: 43-58.

_____. "Eugene Loring Talks to Olga Maynard." *Dance Magazine* July 1966: 35-40.

_____. "Eugene Loring's American Classic." *Dance Magazine* December 1979: 71-75.

Martin, John. *America Dancing.* 1936. New York: Dance Horizons, 1968.

_____. *Introduction to the Dance.* 1939. New York: Dance Horizons, 1965.

_____. *John Martin's Book of the Dance.* New York: Tudor, 1963.

Menotti, Gian Carlo. *Errand Into the Maze.* New York: G. Schirmer, 1947.

Müller, Hedwig. "Jooss and Expressionism." *Jooss: Documentation by Anna and Hermann Markard.* Cologne: Bellet-Buhnen-Verlag, 1985: 12-18.

Nabokov, Ivan and Elizabeth Carmichael. "Balanchine Talks of Music and Related Matters." *Horizon* January 1961: 44-56. Reprinted in *Dance Magazine* October 1961: 42-43, 68.

Newby, Elizabeth A. *A Portrait of the Artist: The Legends of Orpheus and Their Use in Medieval and Renaissance Aesthetics*. New York: Garland, 1987.

Philip, Richard. "Billy the Kid Turns Fifty." *Dance Magazine* November 1988: 36-50.

Pischl, A. J., and Selma Jeanne Cohen, eds. *Dance Perspectives 16: composer/choreographer*. New York: Dance Perspectives, 1963.

Preston-Dunlap, Valerie and Susanne Lahusen, eds. *Schriftanz: A View of German Dance in the Weimar Republic*. London: Dance Books, 1990.

Reich, Steve. "Notes on Music and Dance." *Ballet Review* 4. 5 (1973): 67-71.

Schwab, Gustav. *Gods and Heroes: Myths and Epics of Ancient Greece*. Trans. Olga Marx and Ernst Morwitz. 1946. New York: Pantheon, 1974.

Seashore, Carl E. *In Search of Beauty in Music: A Scientific Approach to Musical Aesthetics*. New York: The Ronald Press Company, 1947.

Siegel, Marcia B. *At the Vanishing Point*. New York: Saturday Review Press, 1972.

_____. "*The Green Table* - sources of a classic." *Dance Research Journal* 21.1 (1989): 16-18.

_____. *Watching the Dance Go By*. Boston: Houghton Mifflin, 1977.

Smith, Julia. *Aaron Copland: His Work and Contribution to American Music*. New York: E. P. Dutton, 1955.

Sorell, Walter. *Dance in its Time*. Garden City: Anchor Press, 1981.

Strauss, Walter A. *Descent and Return: The Orphic Theme in Modern Literature*. Cambridge: Harvard University Press, 1971.

Stravinsky, Igor. *Apollon Musagete*. Revised version. New York: Boosey & Hawkes, 1949.

_____. *Agon*. New York: Boosey & Hawkes, 1957.

_____. "Agon." 1957. Unpublished manuscript tor two pianos. New York: Dance Notation Bureau, n.d.

_____. *Orpheus.* New York: Boosey & Hawkes, 1948.

_____. *Poetics of Music in the Form of Six Lessons.* 1942. Trans. Arthur Knodel and Ingolf Dahl. Cambridge: Harvard University Press, 1970.

_____. *Themes and Conclusions.* London: Faber and Faber, 1972.

Stravinsky, Igor and Robert Craft. *Dialogues and a Diary.* Garden City: Doubleday, 1963.

Stravinsky, Vera. Interview with Genevieve Oswald, 6/14/76. New York City Public Library, Lincoln Center Dance Collection.

Taper, Bernard. *Balanchine: A Biography.* 1960. New York: Macmillan, 1974.

Tatum, Stephen. *Inventing Billy the Kid: Visions of the Outlaw in America, 1881-1981.* Albuquerque: University of New Mexico Press, 1982.

Thornton, Samuel. *Laban's Theory of Movement: A New Perspective.* Boston: Plays, 1971.

Zuck, Barbara A. *A History of Musical Americanism.* Ann Arbor: UMI Research Press, 1980.

INDEX